# The Oboe Concertos of

# SIR WILLIAM HERSCHEL

# The Oboe Concertos of

# SIR WILLIAM HERSCHEL

Edited by Wilbert Davis Jerome

THE AMERICAN PHILOSOPHICAL SOCIETY
PHILADELPHIA
1998

Memoirs
of the
American Philosophical Society
Held at Philadelphia
For Promoting Useful Knowledge
VOLUME 225

ISBN: 0-87169-225-2

US ISSN: 0065-9738

Library of Congress Catalog Card No: 96-96245

# CONTENTS

*For Fran*

# PREFACE

## THE COMPOSER

> My periwig's askew, my ruffle stained
> With grease from my new telescope!
> Ach, to-morrow
> How  Caroline will be vexed, although she
>  Grows
> Almost as bad as I, who cannot leave
> My work-shop for one evening,
> I must give
> One last recital at St. Margaret's,
> And then—farewell to music.[1]

With these words the English poet Alfred Noyes imagined the inmost thoughts of the great scientist Herschel, as he prepared to conduct his last concert before relinquishing a musical career for the pursuit of astronomy.

William Herschel (1738-1822) is the father of modern astronomy. He discovered the planet Uranus in 1781, was the first president of the Royal Astronomical Society, and, upon the recommendation of Benjamin Franklin, became a member of the American Philosophical Society on February 18, 1787. His life and work as an astronomer have been the subject of numerous biographies and studies.[2]  During the first forty years of his life, however, Herschel was a resourceful and respected professional musician, earning his livelihood by composing, teaching, and performing.

Born in Hanover, Germany on November 15, 1738, William was the second son of Isaac Herschel, an oboist in the band of the Hanoverian Foot Guards. Isaac was a man of an enlarged perspective who was determined to give his children the benefit of a broad education. In addition to the basic studies at the garrison school, Isaac instructed his son in the principles of music theory and gave him oboe and violin lessons. William also studied French with an itinerant tutor, Herr Hofschlager. This scholar had a profound interest in scientific subjects, and William's commitment to astronomy later in his life was

---

[1] "William Herschel Conducts," section VI from *Watchers of the Sky* by Alfred Noyes (New York: Frederick A. Stokes, 1912). The late Crawford Greenewalt, former President of the American Philosophical Society, kindly drew my attention to this poem.

[2] The most important documents on his life and works are reproduced in J. L. E. Dreyer's *The Scientific Papers of Sir William Herschel*, London, 1912. The primary source documenting Herschel's transition from professional musician to professional astronomer is Herschel's autobiographical sketch of his life. An account of this manuscript, now at Harvard, is given in Owen Gingerich's "William Herschel's 1784 Autobiography," *Harvard Library Bulletin*, Volume XXXII, Number 1, Winter, 1984.

due, in large measure, to the tutor's encouragement. In 1753 William left the garrison school to take a position as oboist and violinist in the Guards band, but two years later war was declared between England and France, and the Hanoverian King of England ordered the Guards to reinforce the English defenses. Although the Guards stayed only a short time in England, this brief visit was long enough to make a favorable impression on Herschel.

In 1756, Mozart's birthyear, he and his brother Jacob resigned from the Guards band and moved to London, where William found immediate employment as a music copyist. Four years later he was appointed director of the Militia band at Durham. Here he also taught music to members of wealthy families and made important professional connections with many notable musicians including the composers Charles Avison (1709-1770) and John Garth (1722-1810). These were very productive years for Herschel; most of his instrumental works, including symphonies, concertos and sonatas were written in the years between 1759 and 1770. Despite this, the only compositions to appear in print during his lifetime were six sonatas for harpsichord (1769) and his celebrated "echo" catch.[3]

Herschel began a lifelong friendship with the royal family after performing for the Duke of York in 1761. Because of this friendship he received appointments in Leeds in 1762 and in Halifax in 1766. After only three months in Halifax, he was offered the post of organist of the Octagon Chapel in Bath, one of the most important cultural and artistic centers in England. This was too good an offer to refuse, and he took up his post in December of 1766. Herschel did not confine his musicianship to his official duties as organist at the Octagon Chapel; he played the violin in the Bath orchestra and appeared as soloist in many concerts. During a concert in January of 1767, Herschel gave an amazing demonstration of his versatility by performing a concerto for oboe, a concerto for violin, and a sonata for harpsichord.

In 1772 Herschel visited Hanover for the first time since his resignation from the Guards band. He returned to England later that year and was accompanied by his sister Caroline (1750-1848), a soprano of considerable talent. In 1780 Herschel was appointed director of the Bath orchestra, and Caroline often appeared as soprano soloist in her brother's concerts. While neither William nor Caroline could be considered leading virtuosi in an international sense, in their many concerts in Bath they often performed duets for soprano and oboe, like many such singer-oboist duos who toured throughout England and the continent at this time. Franziska and Ludwig Lebrun, and Charles and Mrs. Weichel, whose daughter was the famous soprano Elizabeth Billington, were popular favorites at public and private concerts. In America the most important singer-oboist duo was the Graupners, Johann Christian and Catherine, English expatriates who were popular in Charleston, South Carolina in the last quarter of the eighteenth century.

---

[3]Sterling Murray, *The Symphonies of William Herschel* ( New York: Garland Publishers, 1983), xx.

William and Caroline's collaborative efforts did not end with his entry into the field of astronomy; Caroline later played a critical role in William's career as an astronomer and became a celebrated astronomer herself. She received the Astronomical Society's gold medal on February 8, 1828.

During his tenure in Bath, Herschel turned more and more to astronomy as his principal interest. His astounding discovery in 1781 of Uranus, the first planet to be discovered in recorded history, brought him fame and a fellowship in the Royal Society. The following year the King awarded him an annual pension but stipulated that Herschel was to devote all his time to astronomy. His last professional musical appearance was probably at St. Margaret's Chapel in Bath on May 18, 1782. With his attention now focused completely on astronomy, Herschel proceeded to distinguish himself during his remaining forty years as one of the world's greatest astral explorers. Ironically, it was because of his fame as an astronomer that Herschel was visited by the great musicians who came to England to participate in the international festivals of music in London. In 1791 Haydn came to Oxford to receive an honorary degree of Doctor of Music and visited Herschel at Observatory House near Slough. The celebrated musician Charles Burney (1726-1814) whose writings on music are still greatly admired, considered him to be the perfect embodiment of practical musical ability and scholarly learning, a combination Burney himself tried to emulate. In his honor, Burney wrote a long didactic poem entitled *Poetical History of Astronomy*, of which only a few lines have survived. Herschel died on the 25th of August 1822, the greatest astronomer of his time.

William Herschel the musician is cited in many contemporary references as a performer of exceptional ability on many instruments. One observer, Dr. Edward Miller, noted, "Never before had we heard the concertos of Corelli, Geminiani and Avison, or the overtures (symphonies) of Haydn performed more chastely, or more according to the intention of the composers than by Mr. Herschel."[4] Contrary to the performance practice of his day, Herschel believed that the performer should follow the composer's directions literally. John Marsh, an amateur musician and astronomer, noted in his diaries, "As a true *timist*, Herschel would always adhere strictly to the original tempo, even when performing with the celebrated Tenducci."[5] At this time the great solo oboe virtuosi, Johann Christian Fischer (1733-1800) and Gaetano Besozzi (1727-1794), were the darlings of the English concert circuit, both in London and in provincial cities such as Bath. There is no evidence to suggest that Herschel attempted to promote himself as their equal. Like these performers, however, he would have protected his concertos from piracy by other oboists. One reason for this secrecy was the almost pathological desire by the eighteenth-

---

[4] Edward Miller, *The History and Antiquities of Doncaster and its Vicinity* ( Doncaster, 1804).

[5] Quoted by Lady Suzi Jeans in her *Programme Notes* for a concert in Sussex, August 18, 1970. Giusto Tenducci (b. 1736; d. early 1800s) was a famous castrato noted for his choleric disposition and irregular variations of tempi.

century musical public for constant innovation. A virtuoso brought ever new musical ideas to an eager public. After a concert, the celebrated novelist Fanny Burney commented, "It pained me to hear Cramer and Fischer play so divinely and to so little applause...and especially Fischer, for he is always *new*."[6]

The autograph manuscripts of the three concertos for oboe by Herschel considered here contain precise written directions for many assumed performance practices employed by eighteenth–century oboists. One of these is the *messa da voce*, an expressive device used frequently by singers, consisting of a gradual swelling from *piano* to *fortissimo* to *piano* on a single note. It can be very effective on the oboe, but through overuse, the *messa da voce* soon grew into a grotesque mannerism. On hearing it employed in 1778 by Carlo Besozzi, oboist brother of the aforementioned Gaetano, Mozart's father, Leopold, observed, "This *messa da voce* was too frequent for my taste, and has the same melancholy effect on me as the tones of Dr. Franklin's musical glasses."[7]

The oboe concertos of Herschel the musician cannot be classified as great music in the tradition of Haydn or Mozart, but they are arresting, innovative works, the product of a superb analytic mind driven by an obsession for order and coherence. Stylistically individual and harmonically idiosyncratic, they were written to display Herschel's ingenuity as a composer and his virtuosity as a performer. But Herschel the scientist, with a desire to retain control of all aspects of the interpretation of this music by an unusual abundance of written performance indications, has also given us a useful pedagogical tool in our efforts to recapture something of the musical aesthetic of his time.

## SOURCES

The three solo oboe concertos contained in this volume are from a collection in Herschel's autograph of ten concertos for various instruments acquired by the Music Library of the University of California at Berkeley at the time of the sale of the Herschel family papers in 1958.[8] Of these, the Oboe Concerto in E-flat Major, MS 788 dated 1759, is part of a collection of eight concertos for various instruments assembled by Herschel sometime during his lifetime. The other two complete oboe concertos, MS 787 and MS 789, and a single movement, MS 790, were found separately. The fact that these two latter concertos and the separate movement are scored for horns and bassoons, in addition to the standard complement of strings, suggests that they were written during the years 1760 to

---

[6] *The Diary of Fanny Burney*, ed. Christopher Lloyd ( London, 1948), p. 91.

[7] Emily Anderson, *The Letters of Mozart and His Family* ( London, 1938), II, pp. 798-799. Mozart wrote two chamber works for Benjamin Franklin's ethereal-sounding Glass Harmonica, the Quintet, K. 617 and the solo Adagio, K. 356.

[8] A detailed account of this acquisition and its provenance is given in the late Vincent Duckles' "William F. Herschel's Concertos for Oboe, Viola and Violin," *Festschrift Otto Erich Deutsch* (Kassel, 1963), p. 66.

1762 when Herschel was in charge of music for the Durham Militia band. Accordingly, for this and for stylistic considerations, the editor has designated MS 788 as No.1, and the two C Major concertos, MSS 787 and 789 as Nos. 2 and 3 respectively.

MS 788: Oboe Concerto in E-flat Major.  Score.
I. Allegro  II. Adagio  III. A tempo primo
Inst. 2 violins, viola, bass, continuo
London, 1759

MS 787: Oboe Concerto in C Major. Score and parts.
I. Maestoso  II. Adagio  III. Allegretto
Inst. 2 violins, viola, bass, 2 horns in C
Undated

MS 789: Oboe Concerto in C Major.  Parts.
I. Maestoso  II. Adagio  III. Allegro
Inst. 2 violins, viola, bass, 2 bassoons, 2 horns in C
Undated

MS 790: Movement of an Oboe Concerto in C Major. Score.
Allegro
Inst.  2 violins, viola, cello, 2 horns in C
Undated

## THE MUSIC

### OBOE CONCERTO NO. 1 IN E-FLAT, MS 788

This concerto exhibits many characteristics of the North German *empfindsamer Stil*. The object of this sentimental or "sensitive" style was principally the subjective and direct expression of emotion, and strongly marked dynamic, textural and thematic contrasts. At this time, concertos for oboe and other wind instruments were written in keys that usually had no more than two flats or sharps. With the three flats of E-flat major, it is a difficult key for the eighteenth–century oboe. The performer is required  to employ cross-fingerings which militate against a very fast tempo. Herschel obviously was  aware of this, and, since he prefers the tonal color of this key, his writing provides for a more leisurely and spacious performance aesthestic.

The first movement, *forte* for the first six measures, drops abruptly to *piano* for the next eight, which is followed by a *fortissimo* passage under which Herschel has written *sciolte*, that is, "unconstrained."  Then follows a sudden syncopated figuration dying to *pianissimo*. This short introduction is sprinkled liberally with dynamic accents. Herschel goes harmonically rather far afield in the middle section and must abruptly modulate back to the key of the opening for the recapitulation. The beautifully crafted, long Handelian phrases in the solo part challenge the oboist's control.

Although the second movement, an *Adagio* in C minor, is merely seventeen measures long, Herschel has managed to fill it with as many thematic references from the first movement as he can. Vincent Duckles notes Herschel's obsession with this kind of exaggerated musical coherence and observes that it is akin to Beethoven's approach to structure in which "...melodic, harmonic and rhythmic ideas are used as building blocks, and if the joints are not always smoothly articulated, the general effect is one of power and individuality."[9] The theme of the oboe's first statement of the second movement is related to the opening statement of the first.

The lyrical mood of this movement proceeds without pause into the third, with an opening statement that is a direct quote from the first movement. Amazingly, the final thirteen measures of the last movement are identical with the last thirteen of the opening statement of the first movement. In this concerto, Herschel's dynamic energy and obsession with strangely unprepared modulations are evident everywhere.

## OBOE CONCERTO NO. 2 IN C, MS 787

Whereas the previous Concerto in E-flat clearly exhibited many characteristics of the *empfindsamer Stil*, this one stands in the *galant* tradition. The *galant* style was the standard in England by 1770. It was introduced into English society in the middle of the eighteenth century and exemplified in the concerts of music promoted by J. C. Bach and C. F. Abel in the Hanover Square rooms in London. There were many complaints about the new style, among them that the bass lines were uninteresting, but the new, middle–class public seemed to demand this more homophonic style of composition with a lighter texture and clear, well-defined melodic phrases. The first movement opens with a triadic martial figure followed by a lyrical opening phrase on the oboe. In the more developed middle section, there is much leaping by octaves, obviously designed to display the technical ability of the performer, but of little musical value. The expected cadenza is here fully written out and is remarkably short, with large leaps of a twelfth near the end, reflecting the earlier *motives*.

Herschel seems to be at his musical best in the middle movements of these concertos. In this one, the large intervals of the first movement are transformed into quite elegant passages of melodic invention. The weakness of harmonic invention that seems to plague Herschel in all of his music is less evident in the slow movements, where there are fewer

---

[9] Duckles, op. cit., p. 70.

and more gradual harmonic events. The last movement is a rondo with an appropriately memorable theme. The very short *eingang*, a connecting passage to the final rondo, is fully written out, contrary to contemporary practice.

All three movements in this concerto are in the same key, C major, unlike the two other concertos in which the slow middle movements are in the relative minor. The uniformity of key here is reminiscent of the earlier Baroque suite. But then, Herschel has a long memory, and these concertos are peppered with reflections of the old, and rapidly becoming older, tradition.


## OBOE CONCERTO NO. 3 IN C, MS 789

Unlike the previous concerto in C, which is characteristically *galant* in its conception, Herschel has reverted in this one to the old mixture of "modern" and Baroque stylistic musical elements. It is by far the longest of these concertos, 477 measures, and the weakest in traditional harmonic construction. The first movement has a great deal of what Charles Burney would call "noise in the choruses," by which he meant many dense, busy passages in the ritornellos. There are also many interesting interludes when the oboe plays in dialogue alternately with the entire ensemble or with the violas alone. Herschel often reduces the orchestral texture during the solo work in all of these concertos, occasionally even leaving out the first violins. He has also included in the oboe part of this concerto a separate manuscript with three cadenzas and part of a fourth; in this edition the editor has selected two for the first movement and one for the third. The cadenzas do not appear to bear a thematic relationship to the particular movement, and they were not expected to do so. Some oboe virtuosi, including the celebrated Johann Christian Fischer, whom Herschel heard many times during his tenure in Bath, would carry with them their own cadenzas and insert them in any concerto they happened to be performing.

In the second movement, *Adagio*, Herschel again indicates that the accompaniment should be reduced to single instruments in the slow passages. Because this happens so frequently in these concertos, one is tempted to speculate that Herschel might have had a somewhat delicate tone on the oboe which could easily be overpowered by the strings in the solo passages. It is well documented that the tone produced by eighteenth-century oboists varied greatly from powerful and robust in the case of the Italian virtuosi to sweet and "melting" in the hands of the French and English performers. Fanny Burney mentions to her sister Susan on July 23, 1786, that, at a concert on the evening of that day, "the sweet-flowing, melting, celestial notes of Fischer's hautbois...made the evening pass so *smoothingly*, I could listen to nothing else."[10]

---

[10]*The Diary of Fanny Burney*, op. cit., p. 114. Mozart had a very different opinion of Fischer's tone and composition when he heard him in Vienna in 1787. Writing to his father on April 4 of that year he says, "And then his concertos of his own composition! Every ritornello lasts a quarter of an hour—then enters

The last movement, in duple meter, employs a mannerism taken over from the eighteenth century Venetian operatic aria, known as the "motto beginning" or *Devise*. It is a statement of the melody played at the outset of the movement by the soloist, which is then followed by an instrumental ritornello until the return of the "true" entrance of the soloist. Beginning as a mannerism to attract attention to the soloist, it was later incorporated into the oboe concerto as an effective musical device. Especially intriguing in this movement is the great number of ways that the composer has combined the solo oboe with other solo instruments of the orchestra after the manner of a musical dialogue.

### MOVEMENT OF AN OBOE CONCERTO, MS 790

This separate movement clearly has strong thematic relationships to the first two movements of the previous concerto. Its rondo theme and the opening statement of the first movement of concerto MS 789 are distinctly similar. Additionally, it is, like the last two movements of the previous concerto, in triple meter. It is quite possible that this movement may be the original final movement of MS 789.

---

the hero—lifts up one leaden foot after another, and plumps them down on the ground alternately. His tone is all through his nose, and his tenuto is like the tremulant stop on the organ." Emily Anderson, op. cit., p. 77.

# ACKNOWLEDGMENTS

The editor wishes to thank John Roberts, Head Music Librarian, the University of California, Berkeley for permitting access to the Herschel manuscripts on which this edition is based. I am also grateful to Owen Gingerich, Professor of Astronomy and of the History of Science, Smithsonian Astrophysical Observatory and Harvard College Observatory, who first drew my attention to Herschel's music and has shared with me his encyclopedic knowledge of the Herschel chronicle. I also thank Sterling Murray, Professor of Music at West Chester University for sharing his expert knowledge of Herschel the musician with me. His groundbreaking study of the Symphonies of Herschel has been of immense help during this project. I acknowledge a special debt to the late and much beloved former President of the American Philosophical Society, Crawford Greenewalt, who gave his characteristic enthusiasm and encouragement to this project. To Carole LeFaivre-Rochester I give my thanks for her gracious editorial wisdom in the preparation of this edition. Finally, I thank my dear wife, Frances, who not only supervised this edition with her insightful musical intelligence, but also was my co-worker in the preparation of the scores.

The premiere recording of the Oboe Concertos No.1 in E-flat and No.2 in C of Herschel was made in August of 1996 by Richard Woodhams, Principal Oboist of The Philadelphia Orchestra with The Mozart Orchestra of Philadelphia, Davis Jerome, conductor: *Sir William Herschel: Music by the Father of Modern Astronomy.* Newport Classic, CD NPD 85612.

FACSIMILES OF VARIOUS PAGES OF THE AUTOGRAPH

MANUSCRIPTS OF THE OBOE CONCERTOS

1. First violin part of the second movement of Oboe Concerto No. 2 in C from the autograph MS.787 in the Music Library of the University of California, Berkeley, page 1.

2. Cadenzas for movements 1 and 2 of Oboe Concerto No. 2 in C from the autograph MS. 787 in the Music Library of the University of California, Berkeley, page 26.

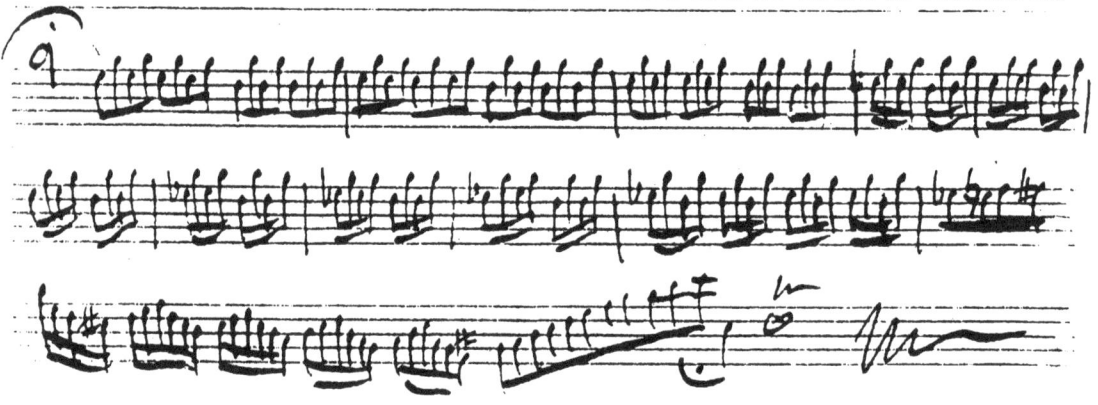

3. Cadenzas for movement I of Oboe Concerto No. 3, in C from the autograph MS. 789 in the Music Library of the University of California, Berkeley, page 24.

4. Movement of an Oboe Concerto in C from the autograph MS. 790 in the Music
Library of the University of California, Berkeley, pages 1-3.

*The Oboe Concertos of Sir William Herschel*

# Herschel Oboe Concertos

*The Oboe Concertos of Sir William Herschel*

# CONCERTO NO. 1 IN E-FLAT

William Herschel

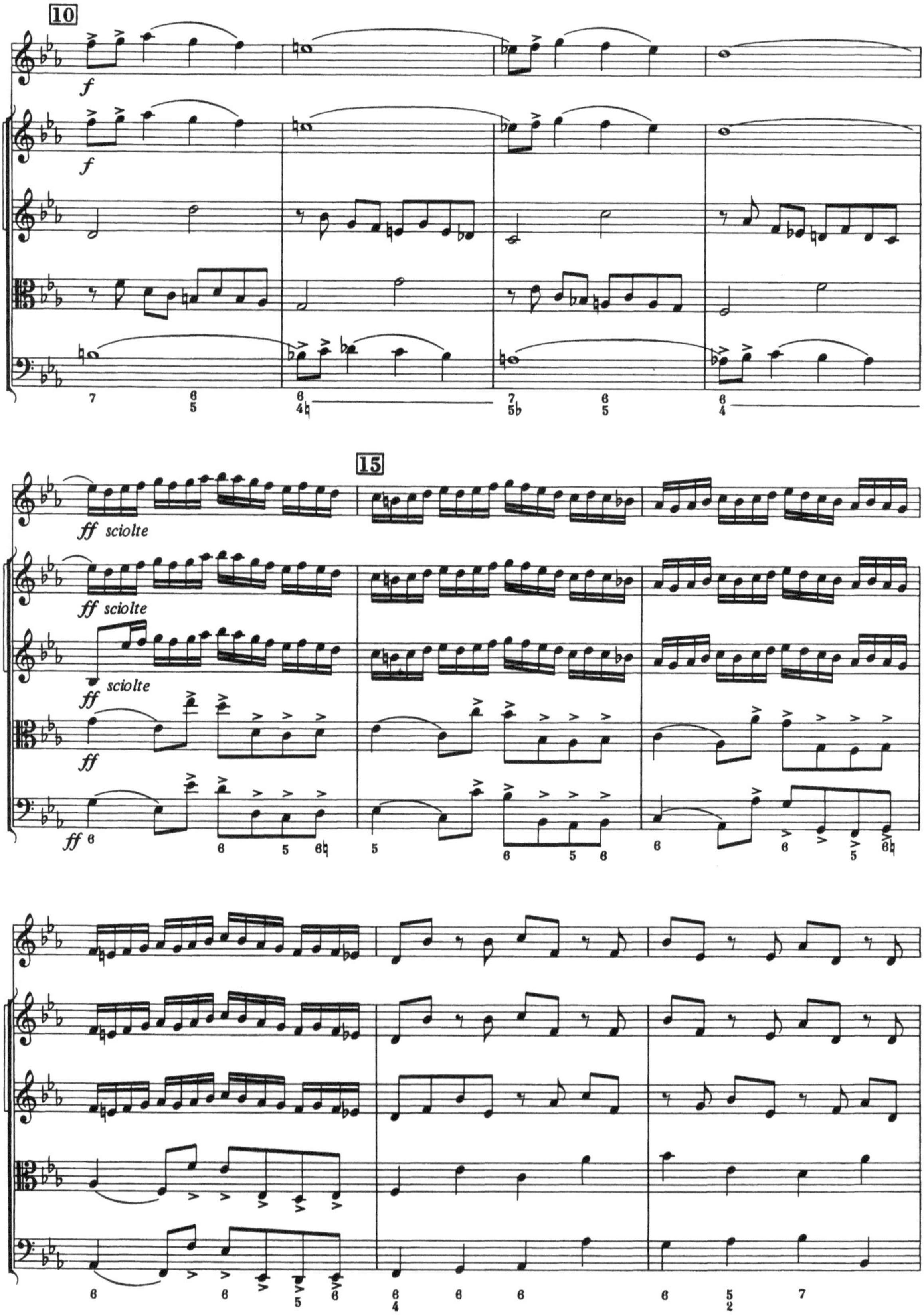
10
f
f
15
ff sciolte
ff sciolte
sciolte
ff
ff
ff

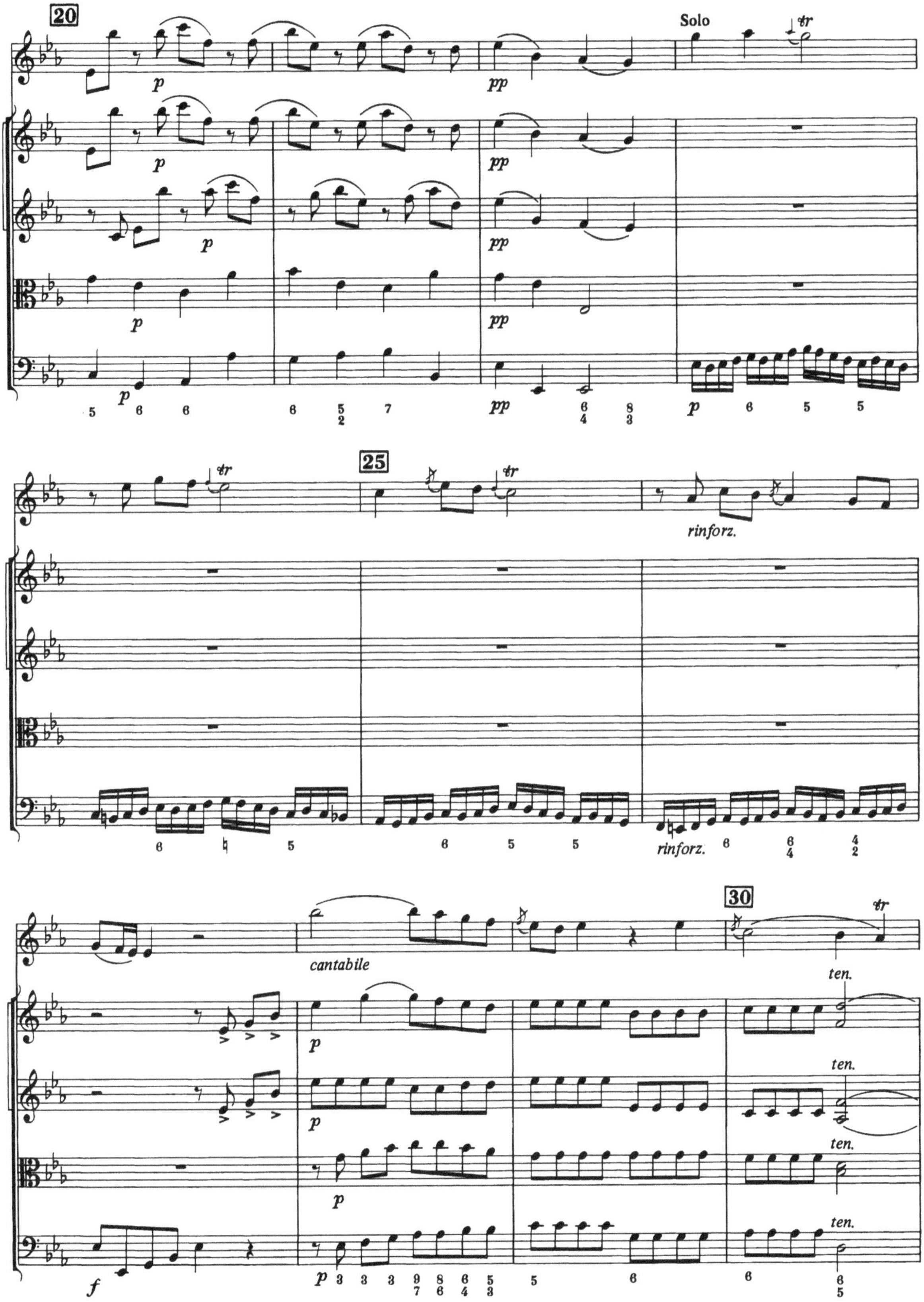
20
Solo
tr
p
pp
25
rinforz.
30
cantabile
ten.
f

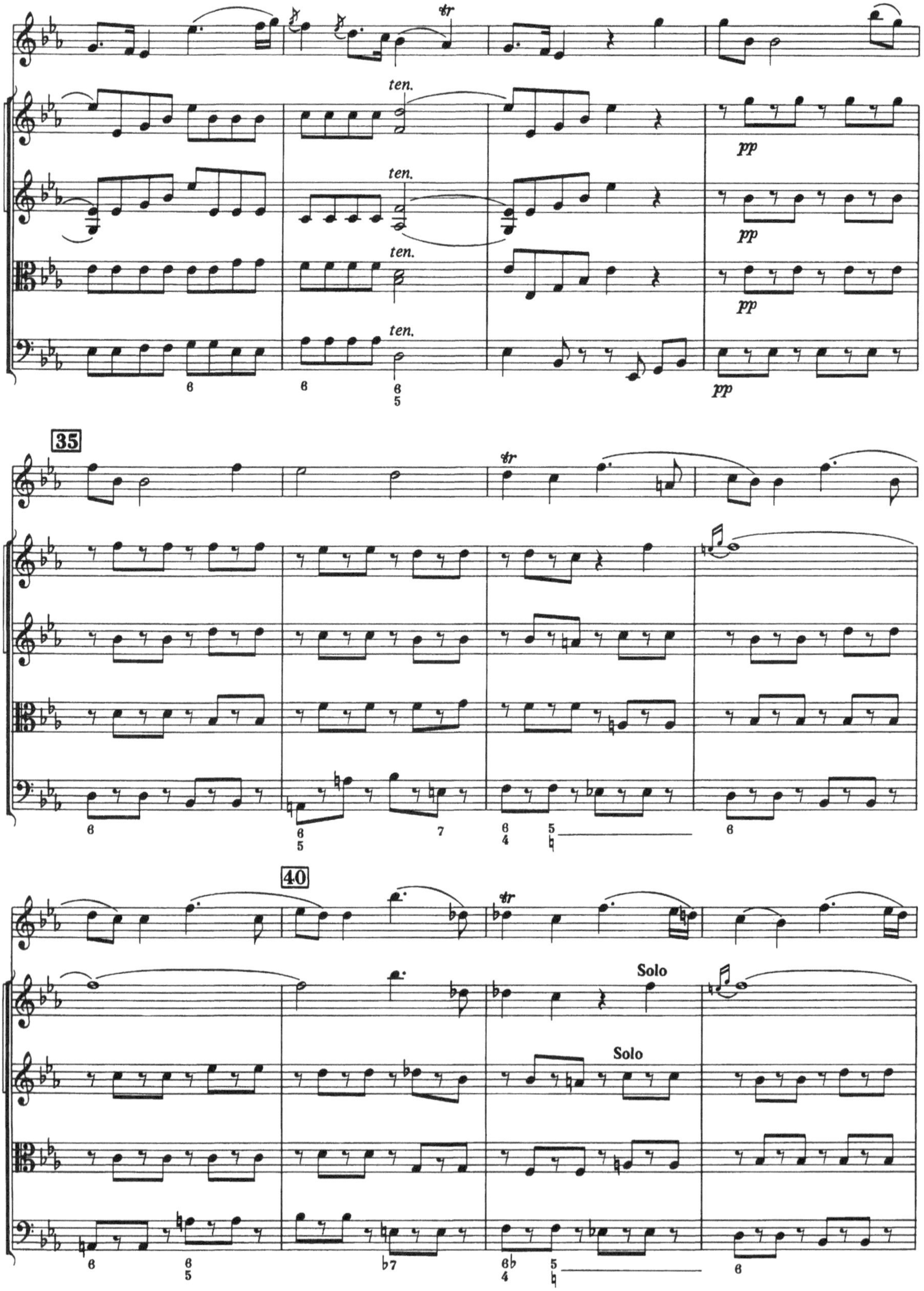
tr
ten.
ten.
ten.
ten.
pp
pp
pp
pp
35
tr
40
tr
Solo
Solo

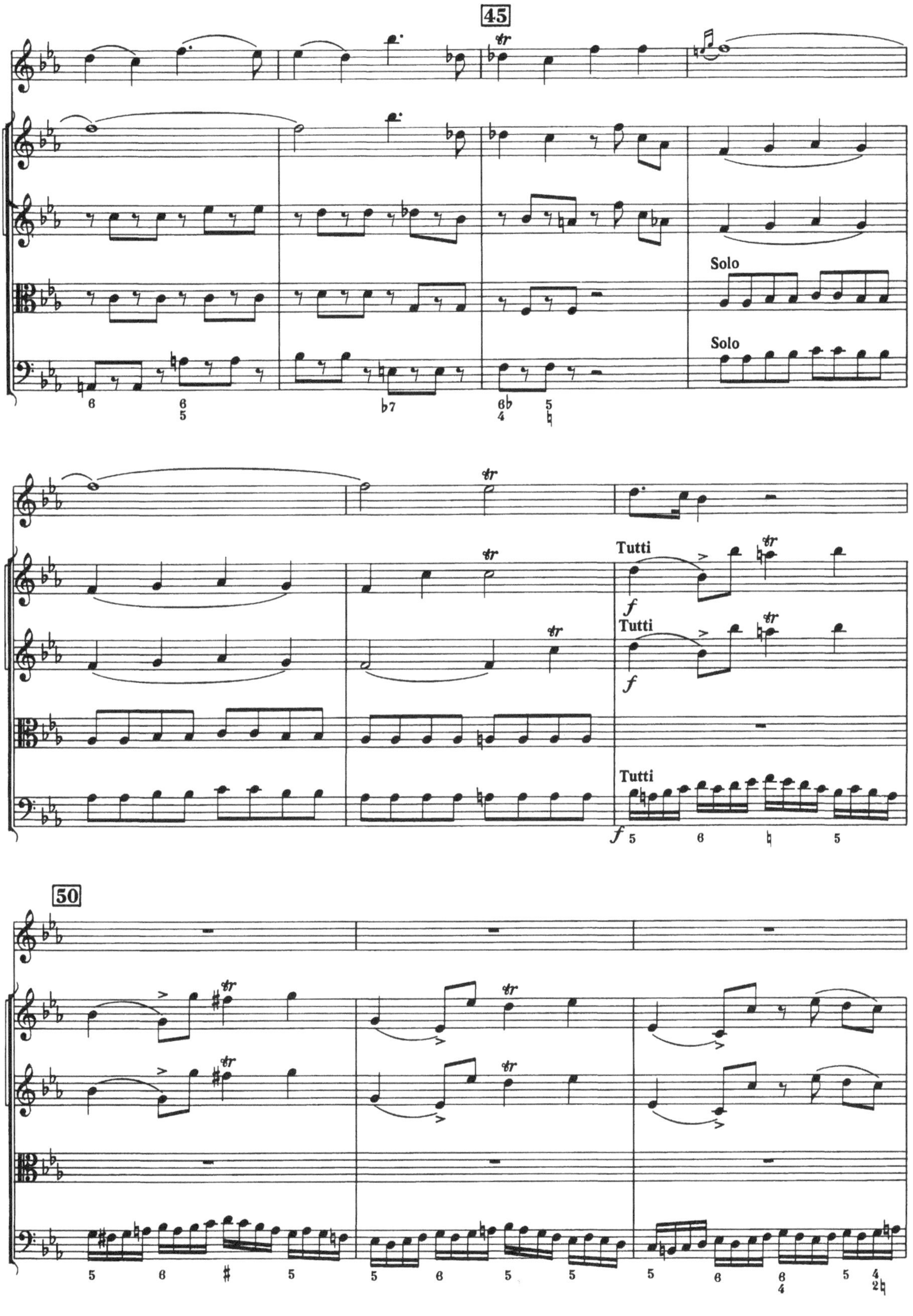
45
Solo
Solo
Tutti
Tutti
Tutti
50

6

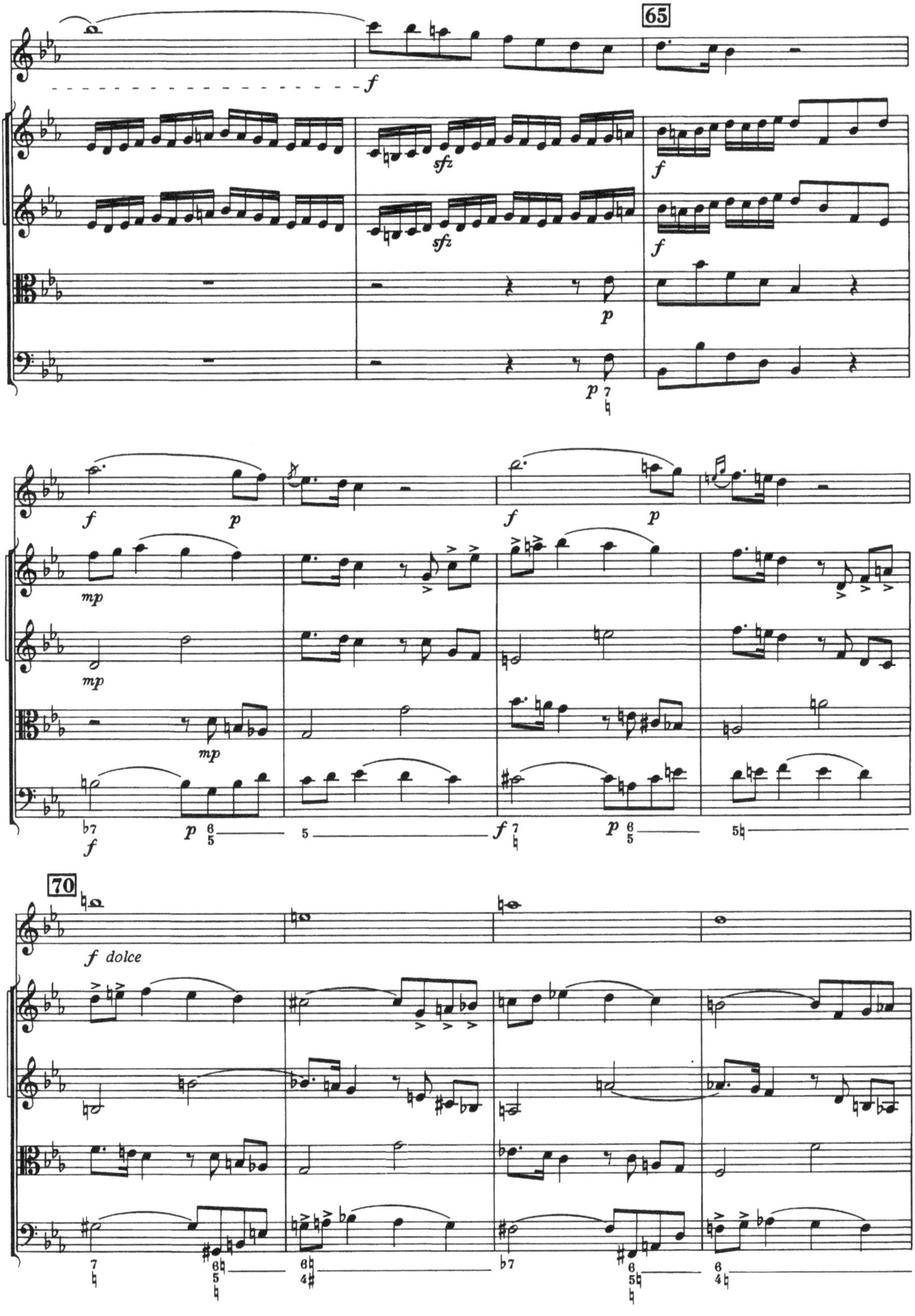
65
70
f dolce

8

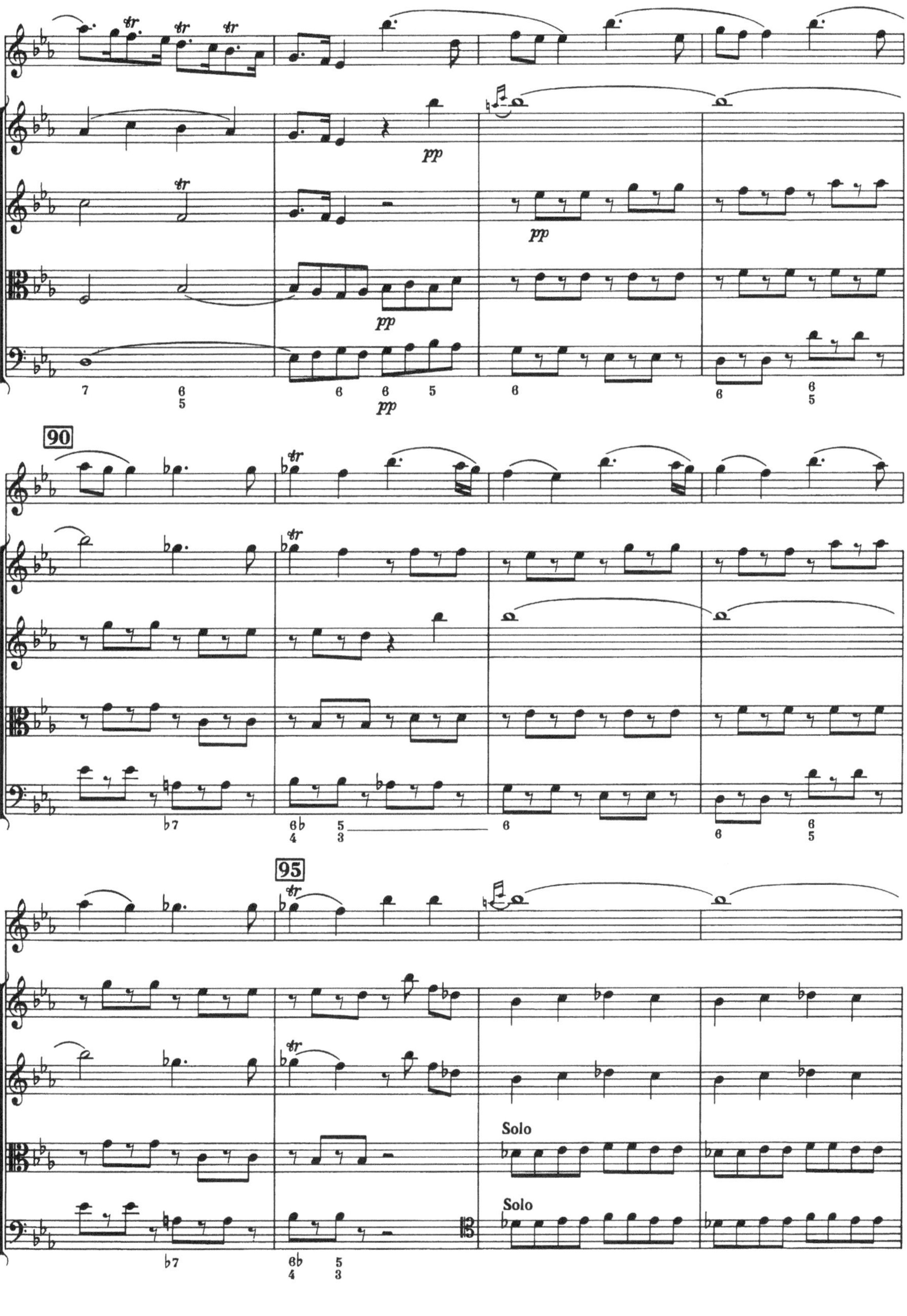
pp
pp
pp
pp
90
95
Solo
Solo

10

William Herschel

# ADAGIO

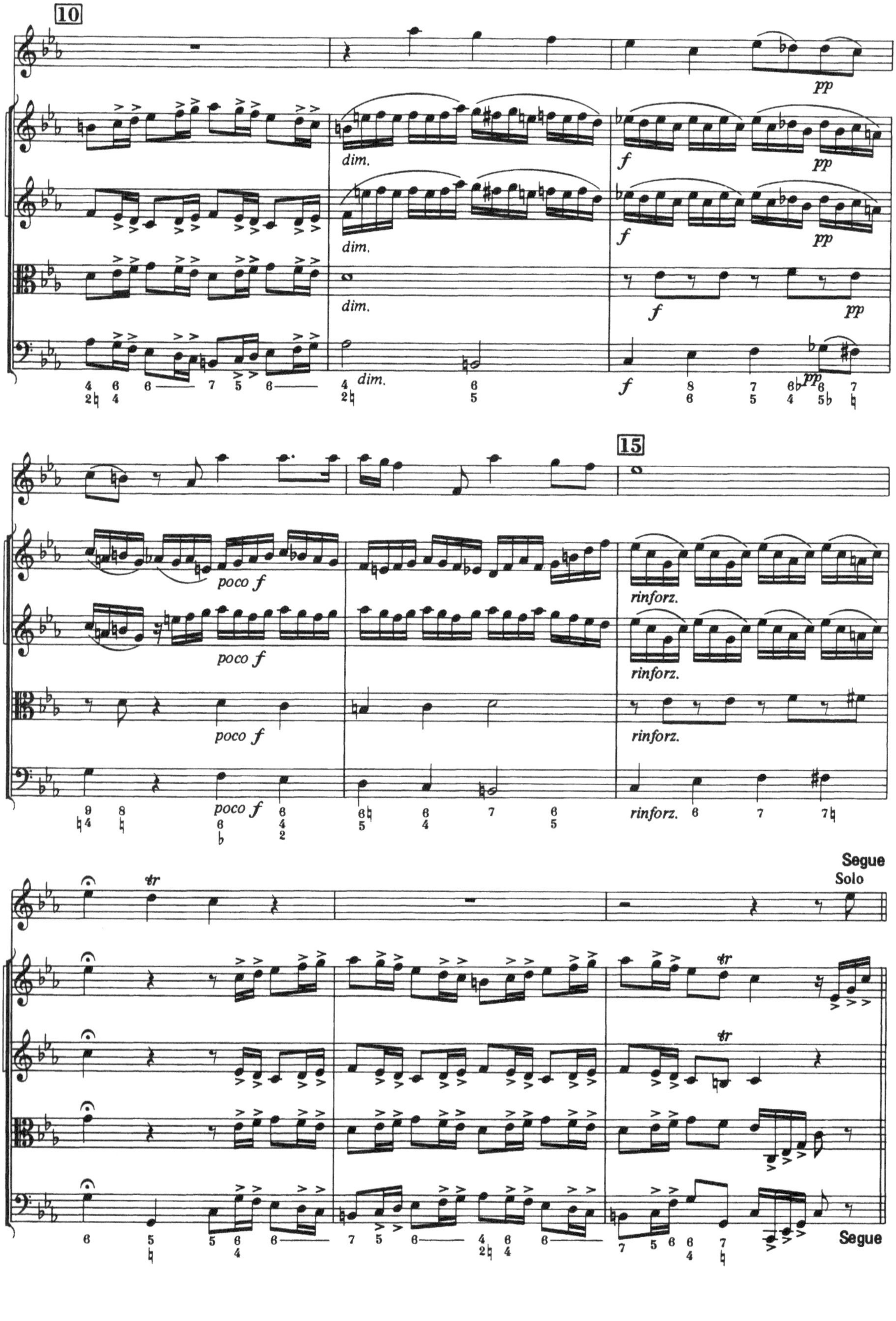
10
pp
dim.
f
dim.
pp
f
pp
15
poco f
rinforz.
Segue
Solo
tr
Segue

**A Tempo Primo**

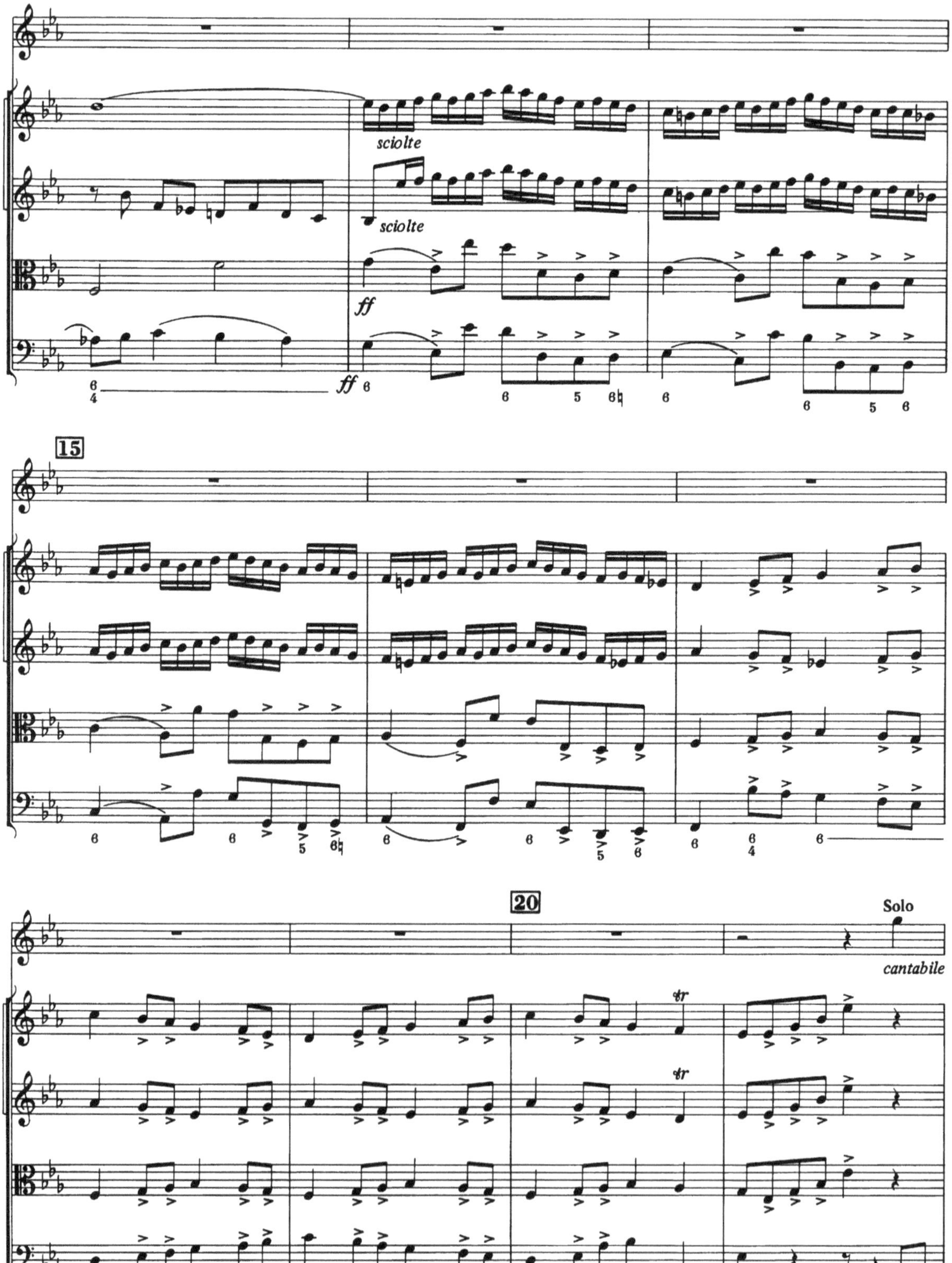
sciolte
sciolte
ff
ff
15
20
Solo
cantabile
tr
tr

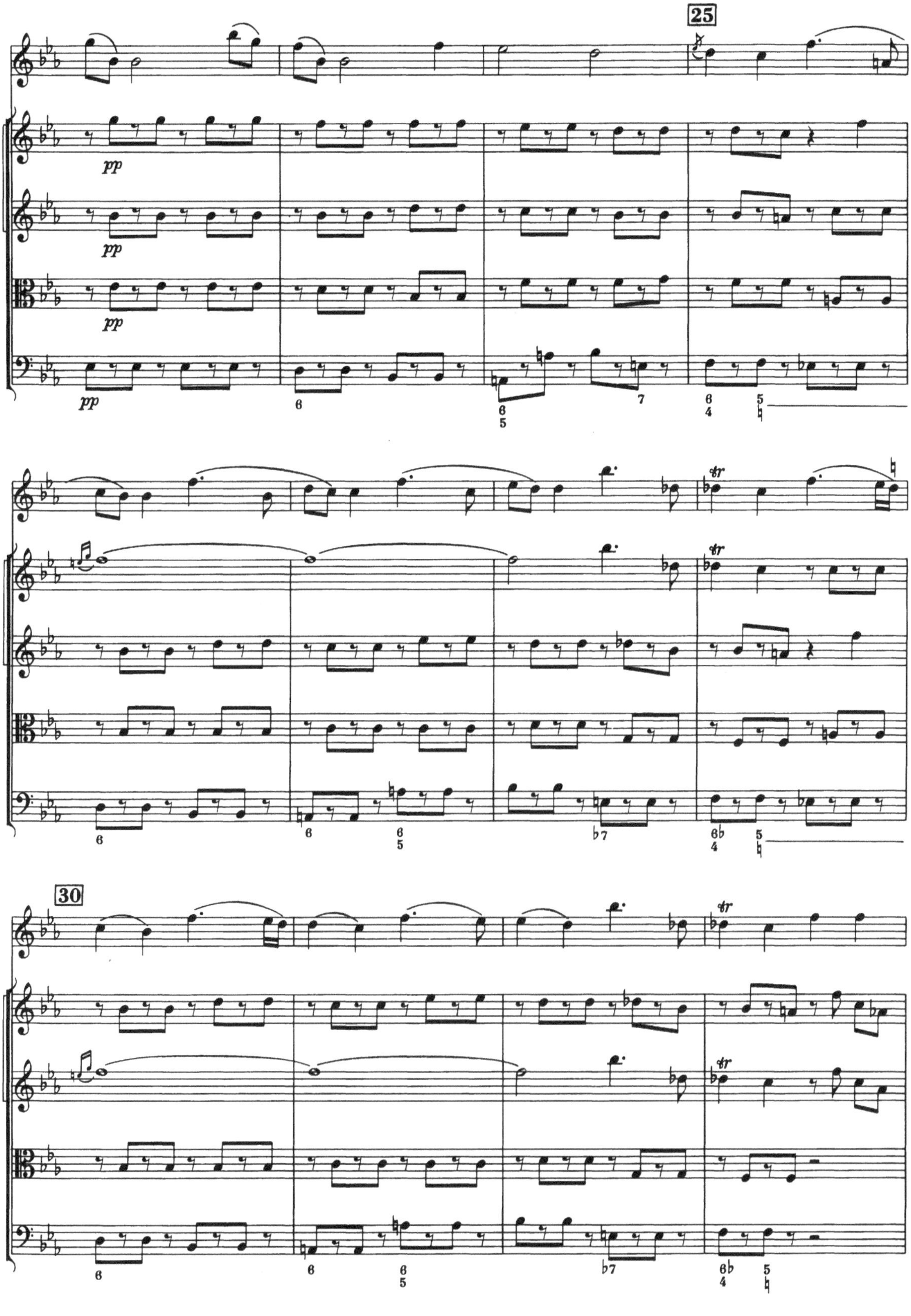
25
pp
pp
pp
pp
tr
30
tr

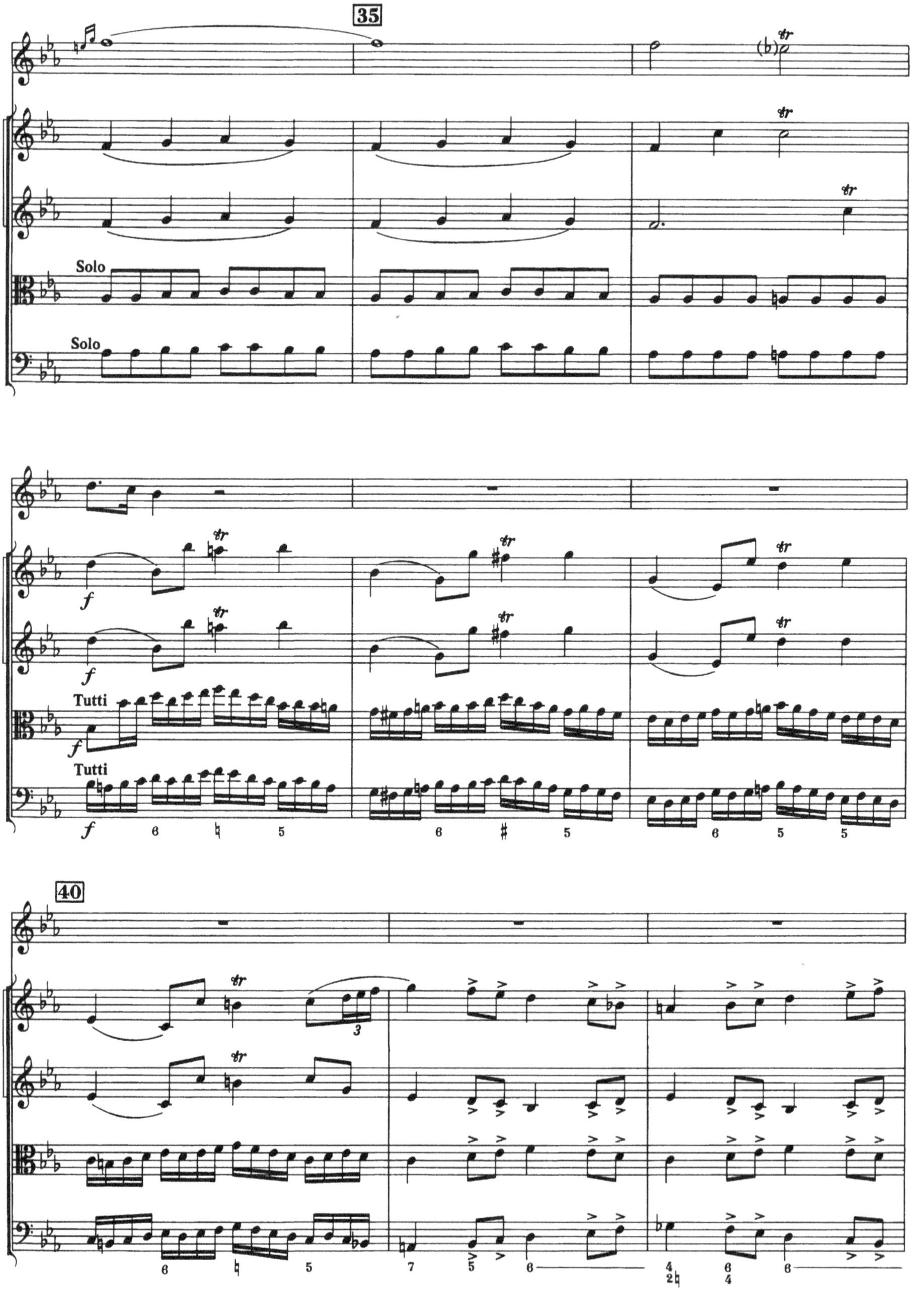
35
Solo
Solo
Tutti
Tutti
40

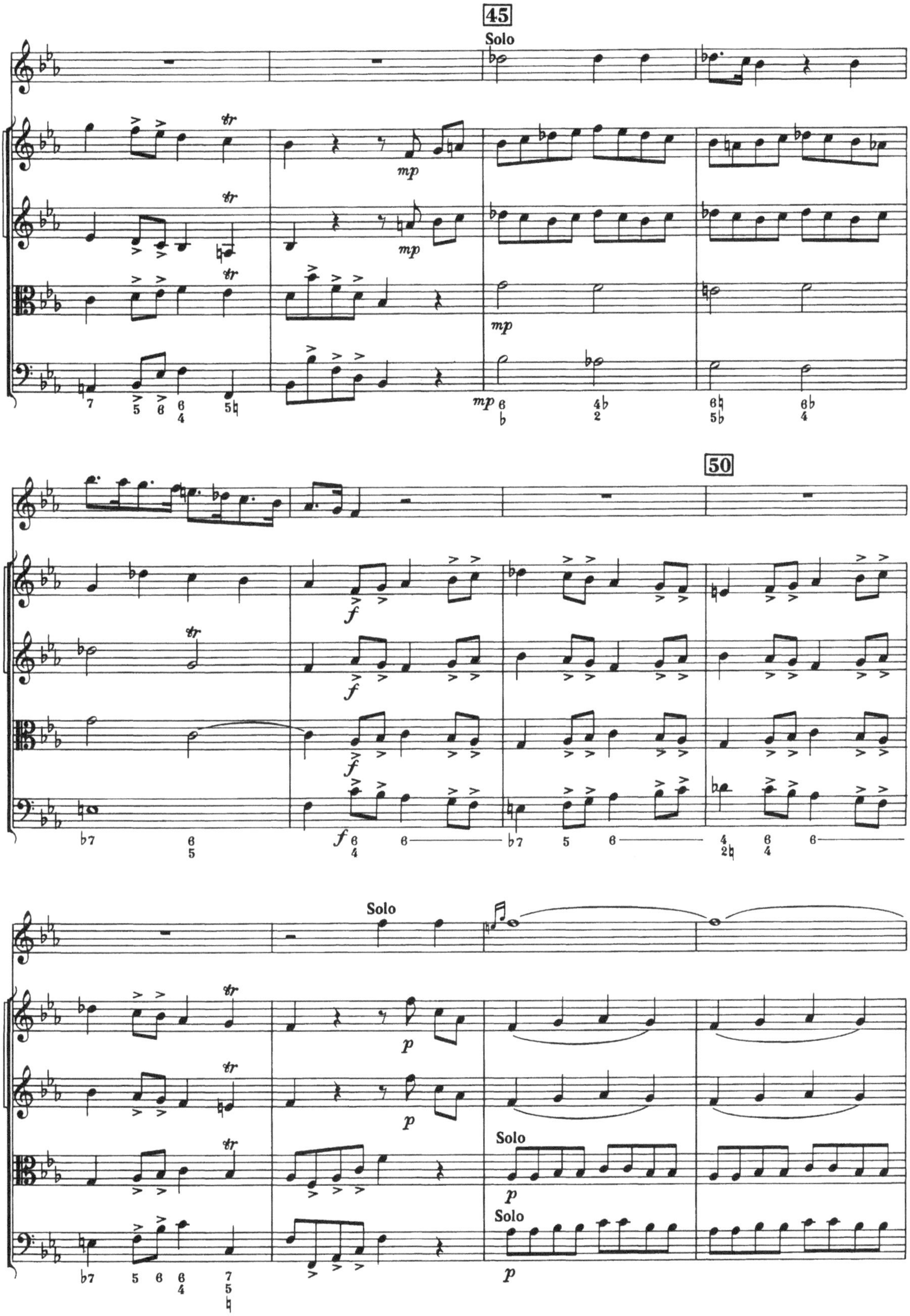
45
Solo
mp
50
f
Solo
p
Solo
p
Solo
p

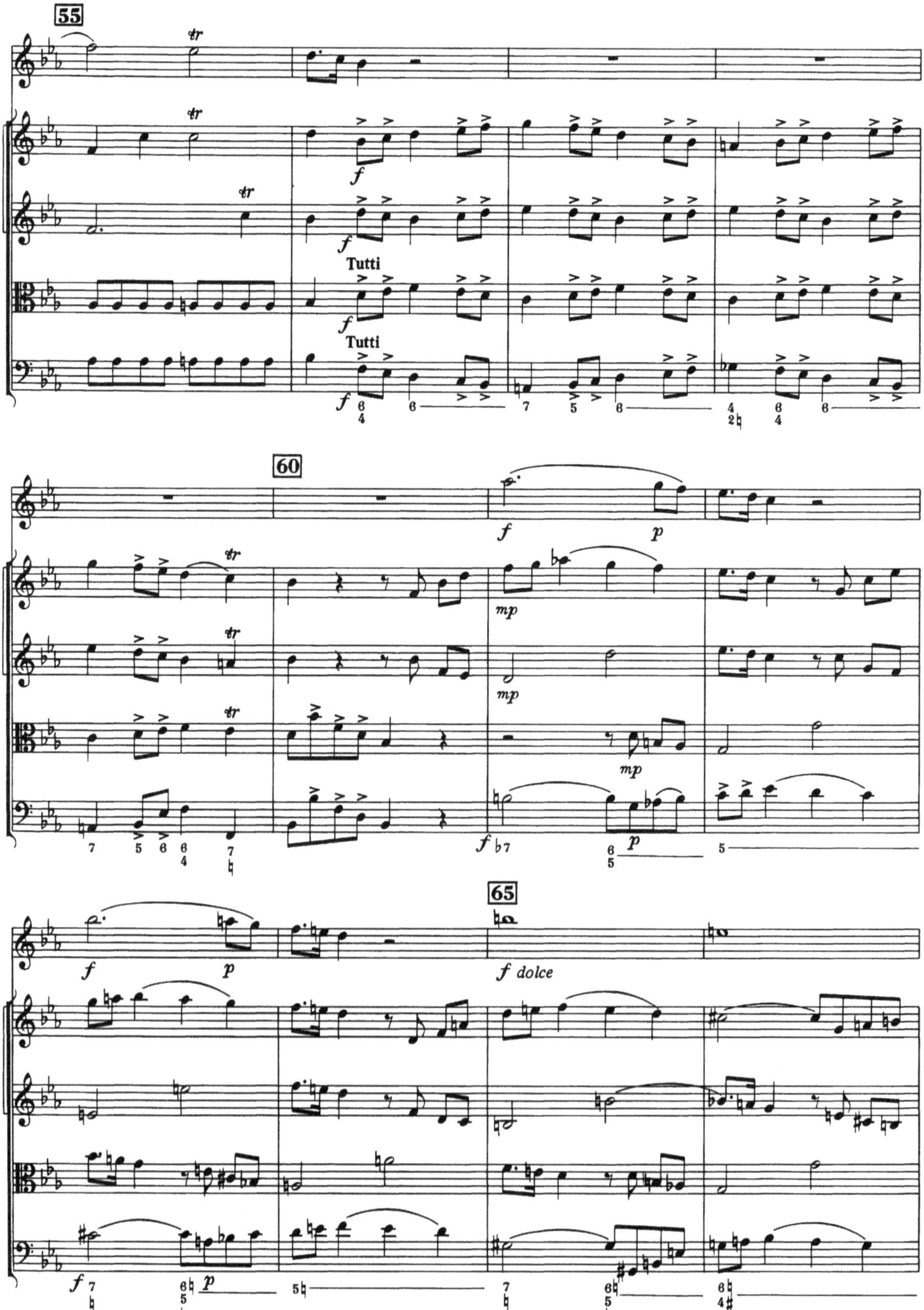
55
tr
f
Tutti
60
mp
p
65
f dolce

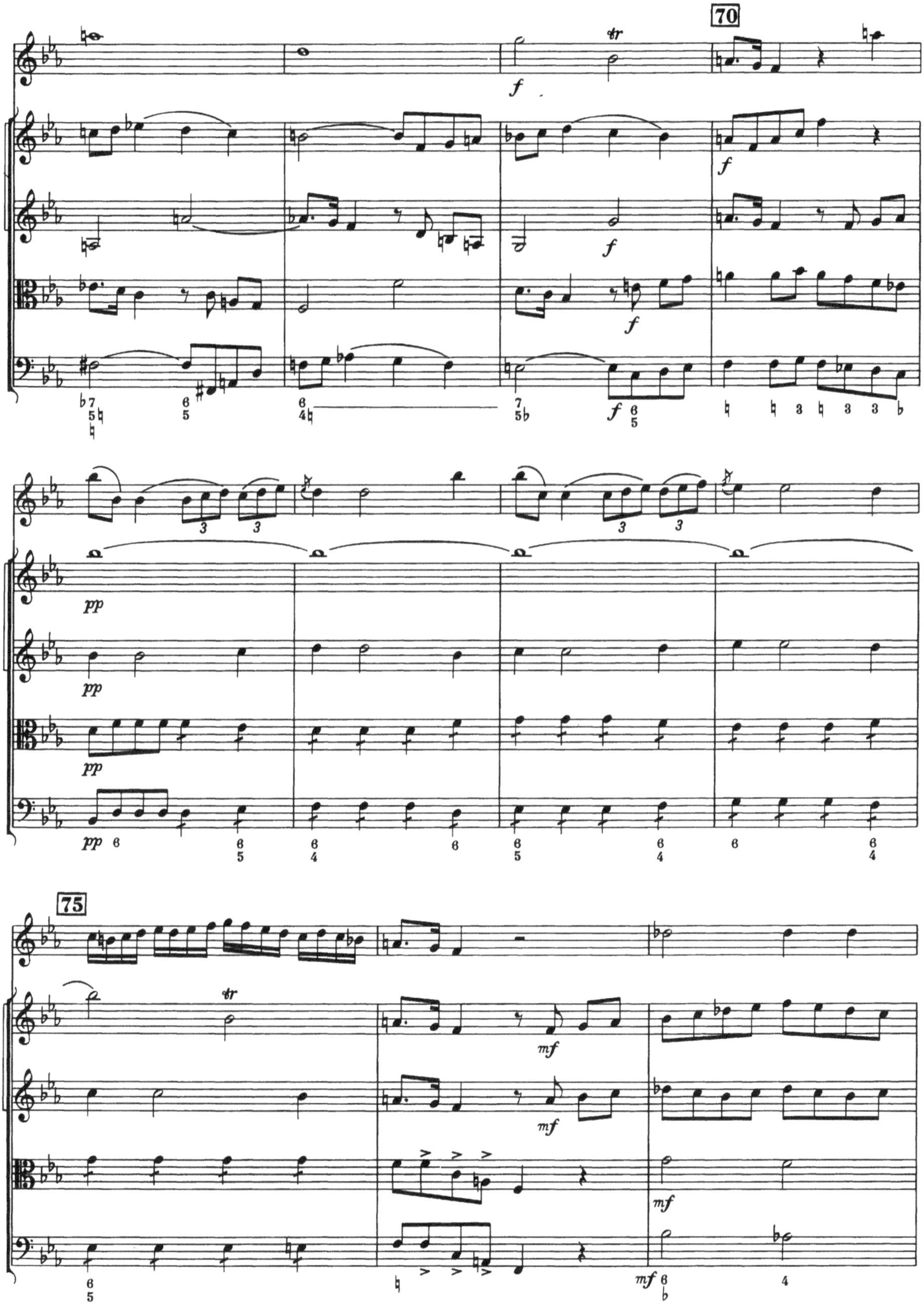
70
tr
f
pp
75
mf

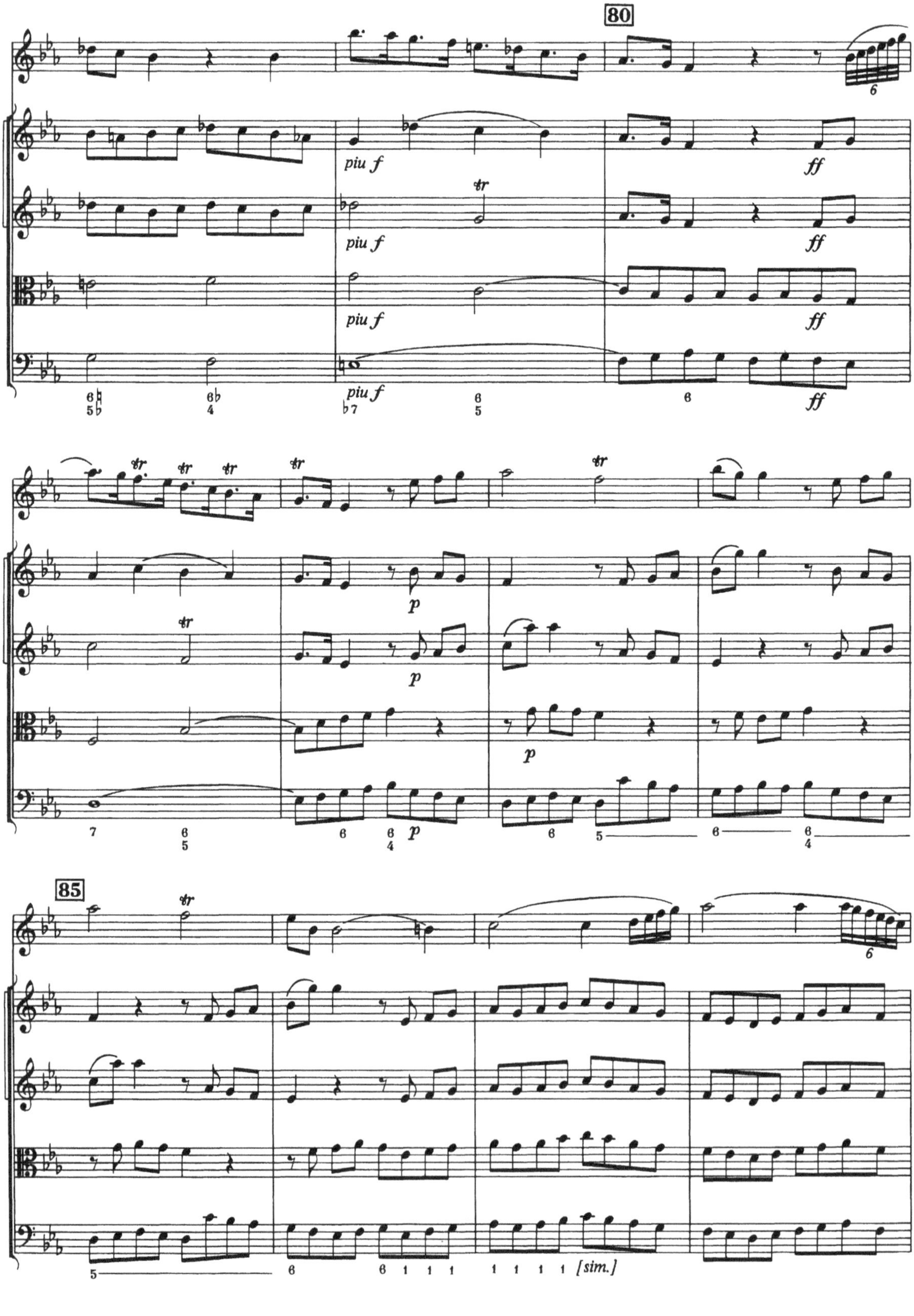
80
piu f
ff
p
85
[sim.]

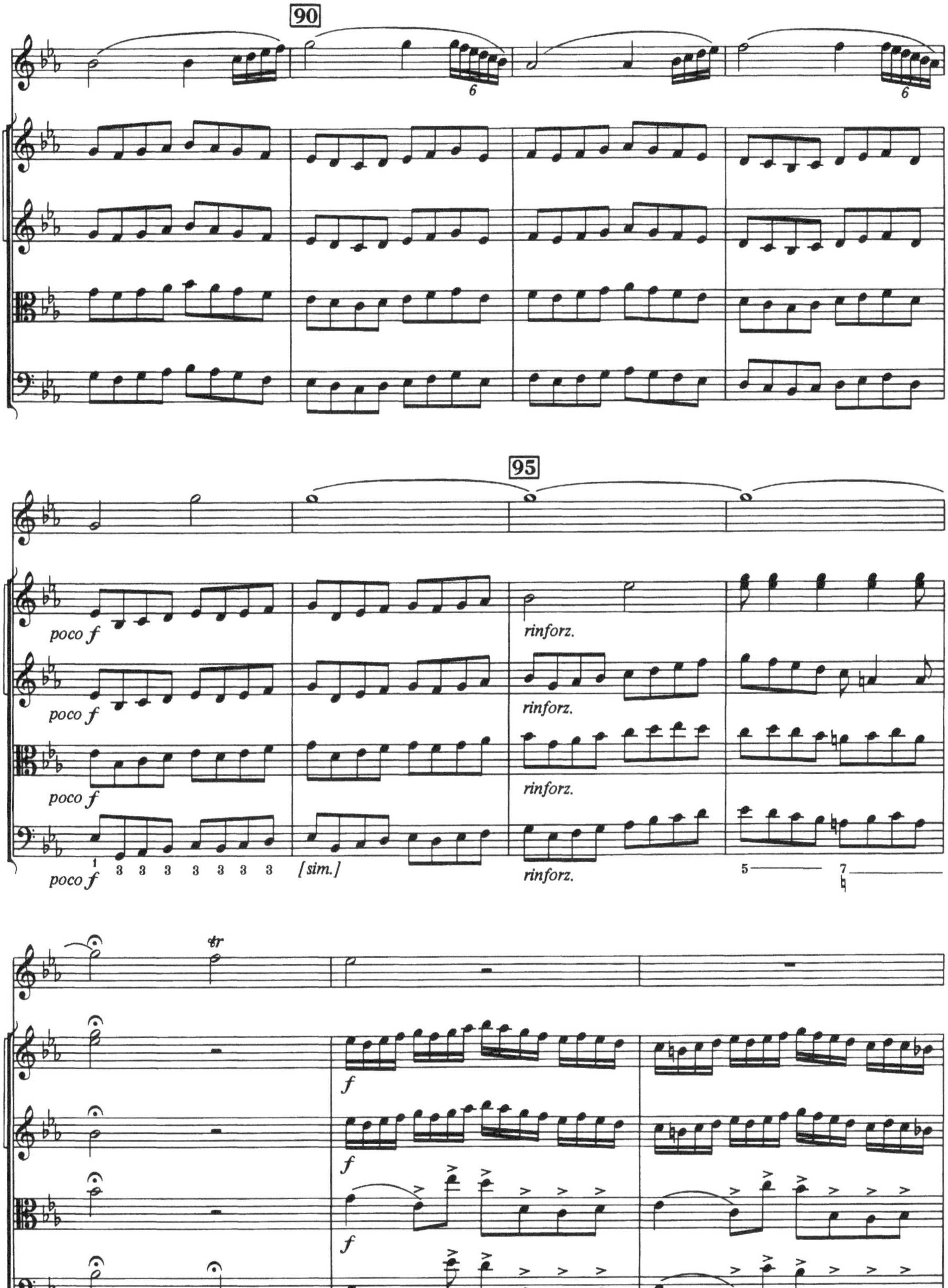

90
95
poco f
rinforz.
[sim.]
tr
f

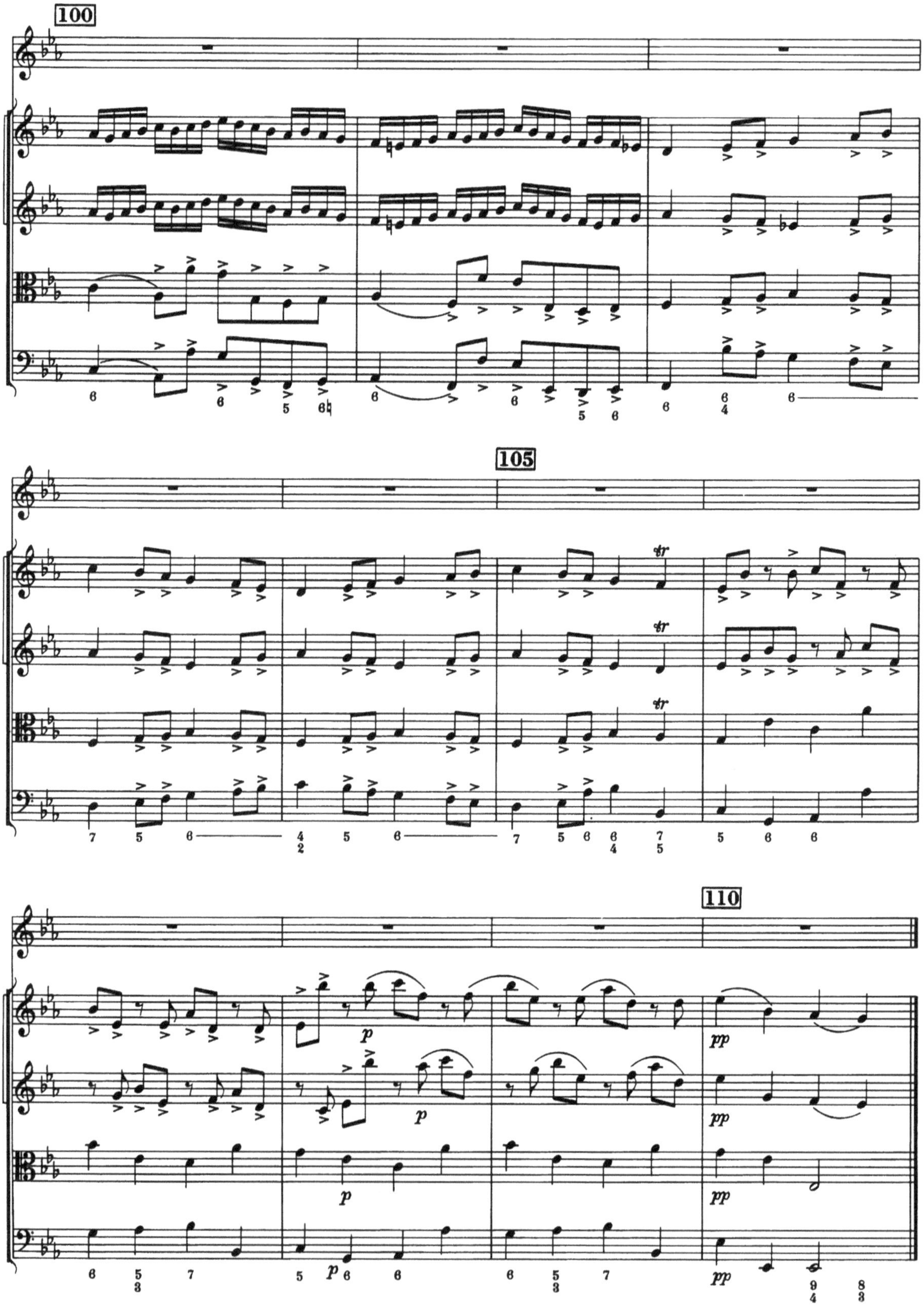


London, 1759

# CONCERTO NO. 2 IN C

William Herschel

## I

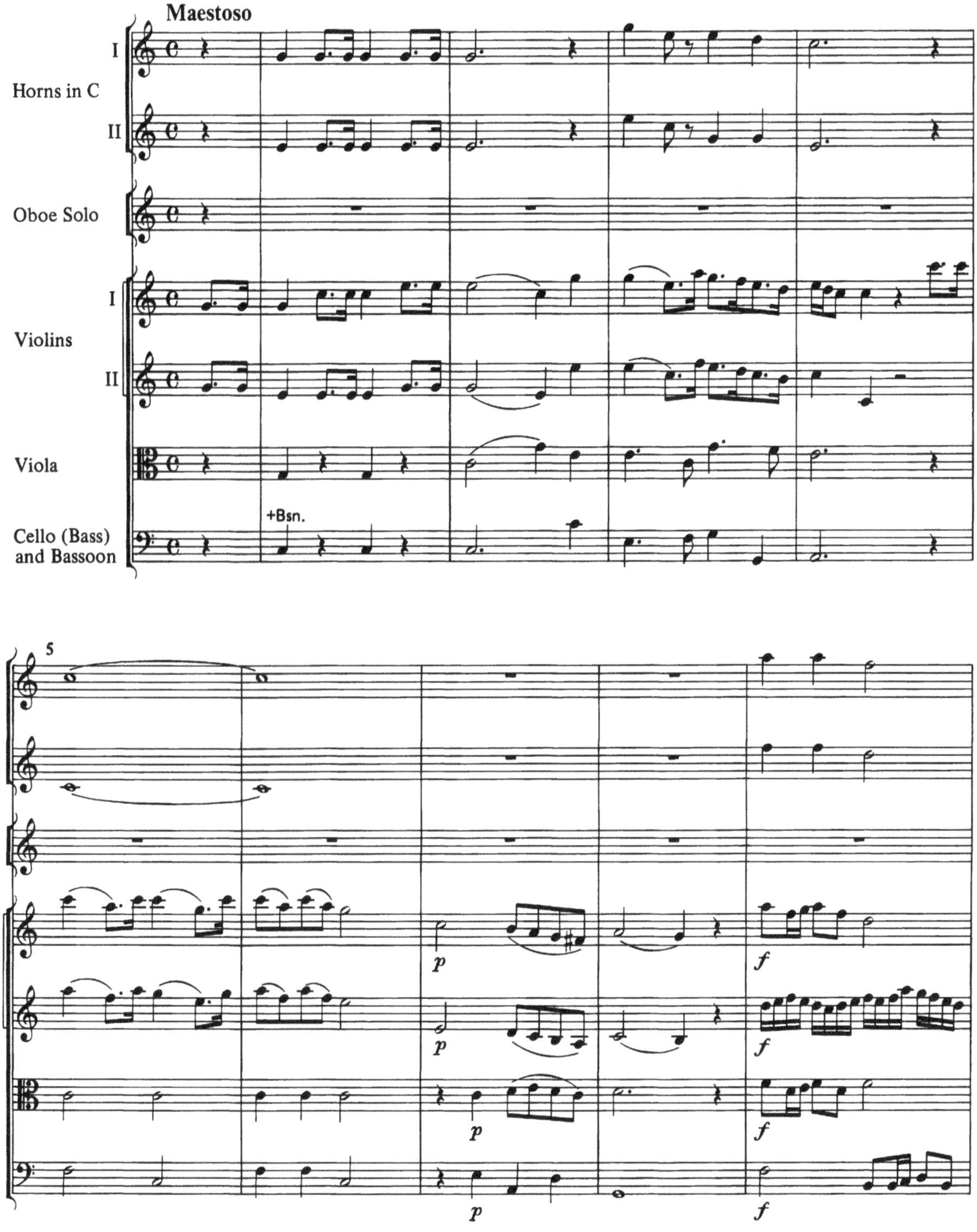

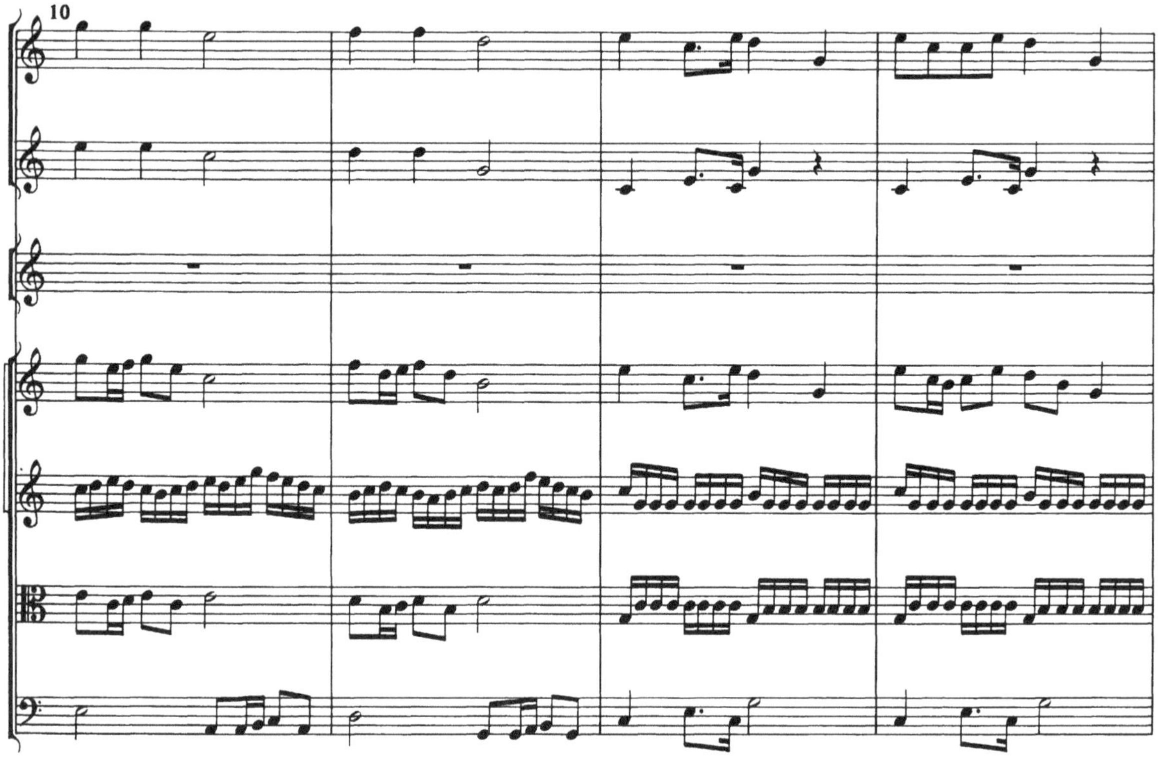
10

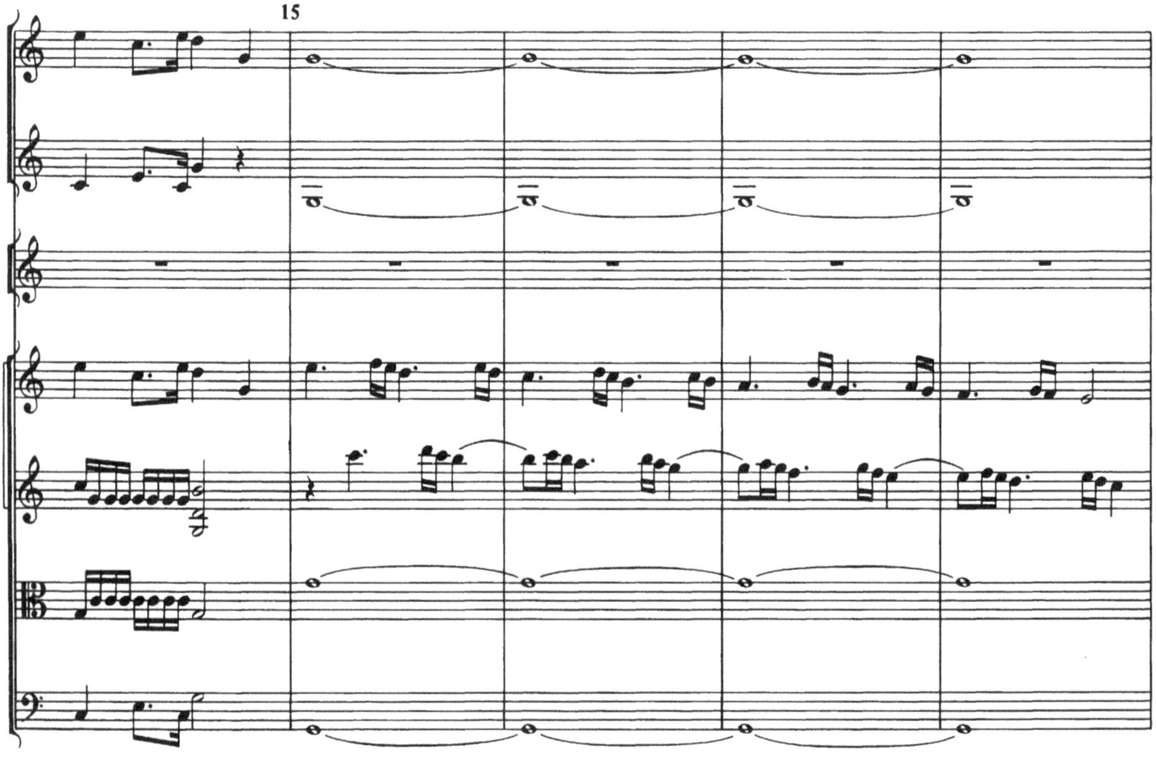
15

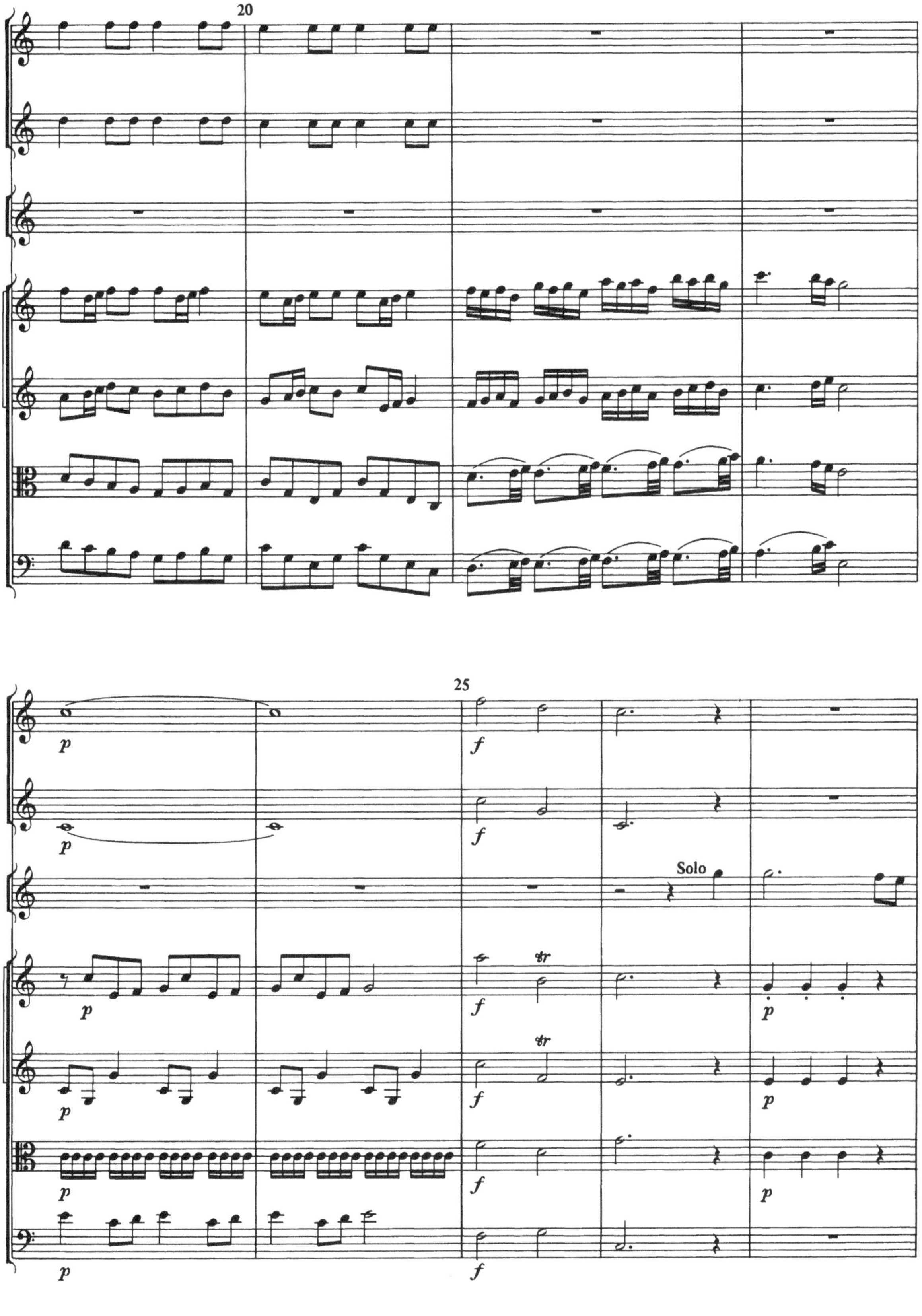
20
25
Solo

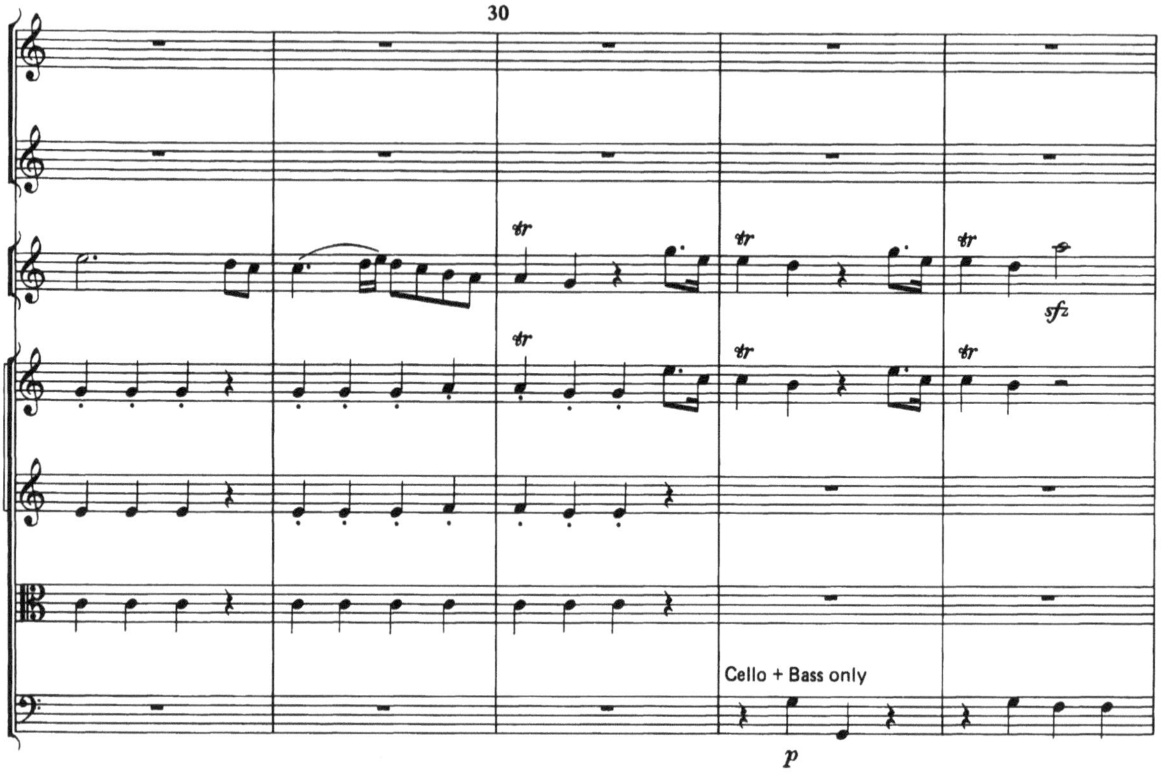
30
tr
sfz
Cello + Bass only
p

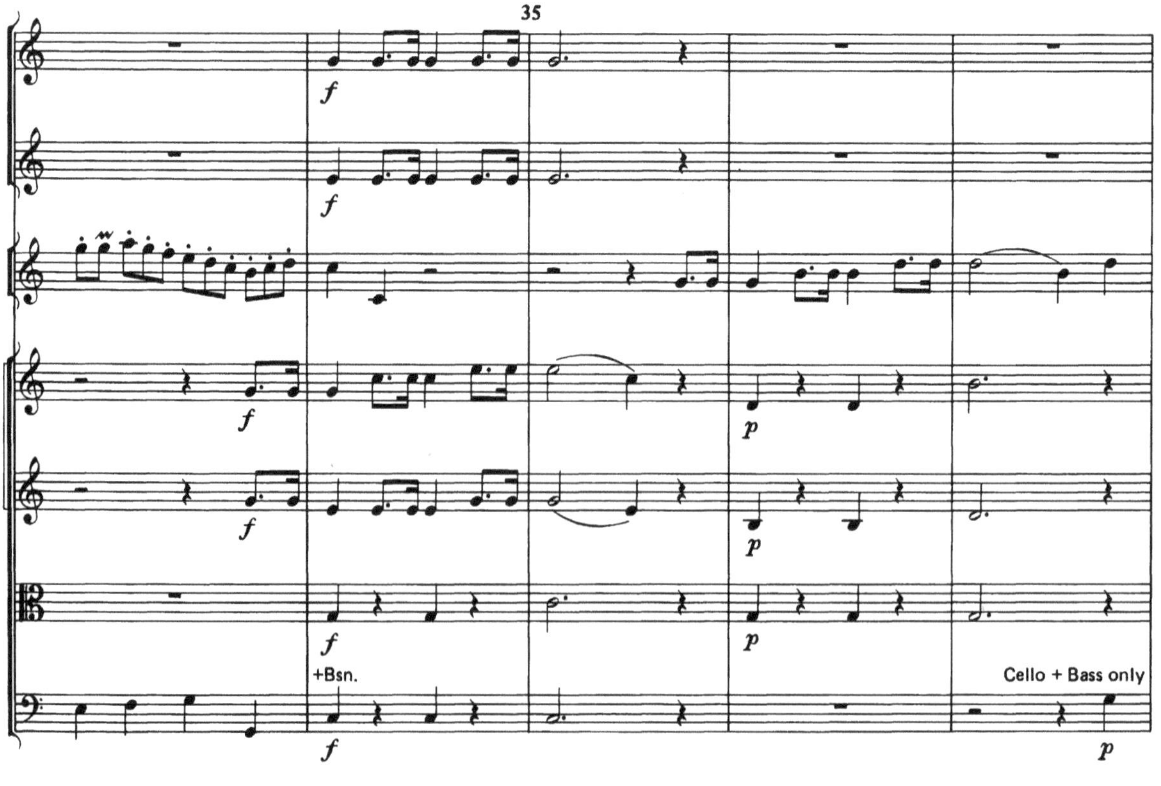
35
f
p
+Bsn.
Cello + Bass only

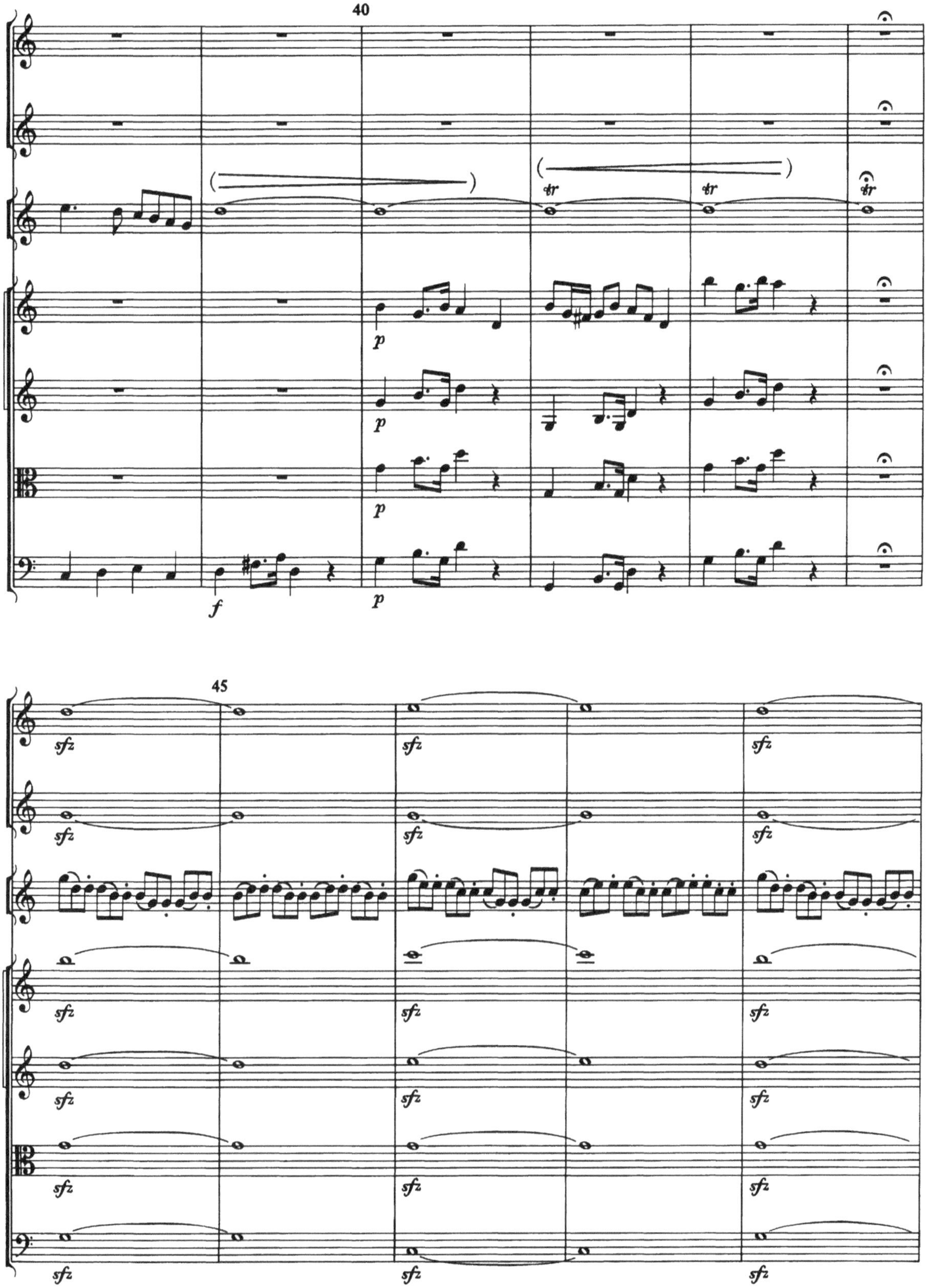
40
45
tr
p
f
sfz

* Version in oboe part:

60

Cello + Bass only

+Bsn.

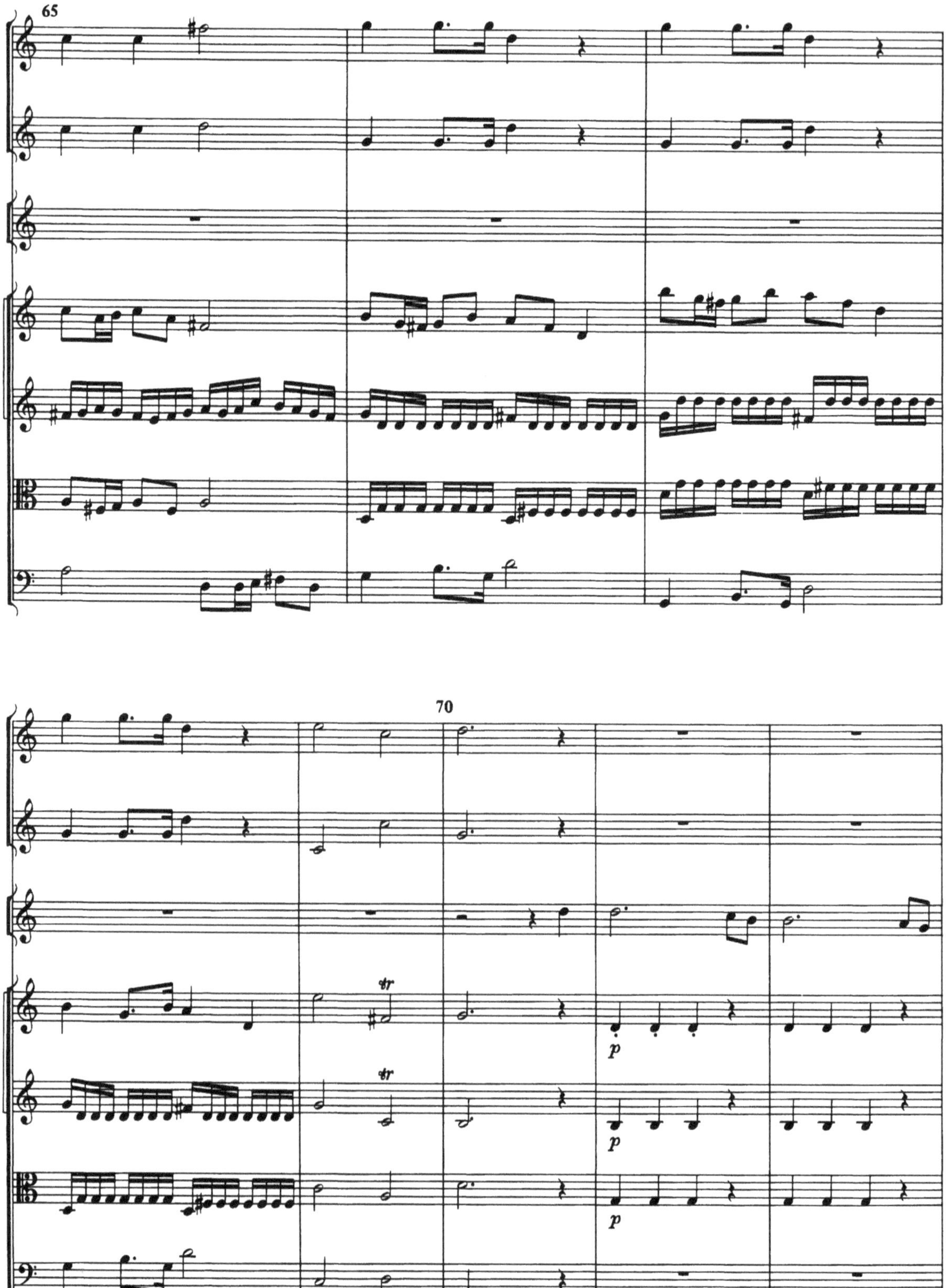
65
70
tr
tr
p
p
p

75
Cello + Bass only
p
f
80
p
f
p cresc.
p cresc.
p cresc.
p cresc.
p cresc.

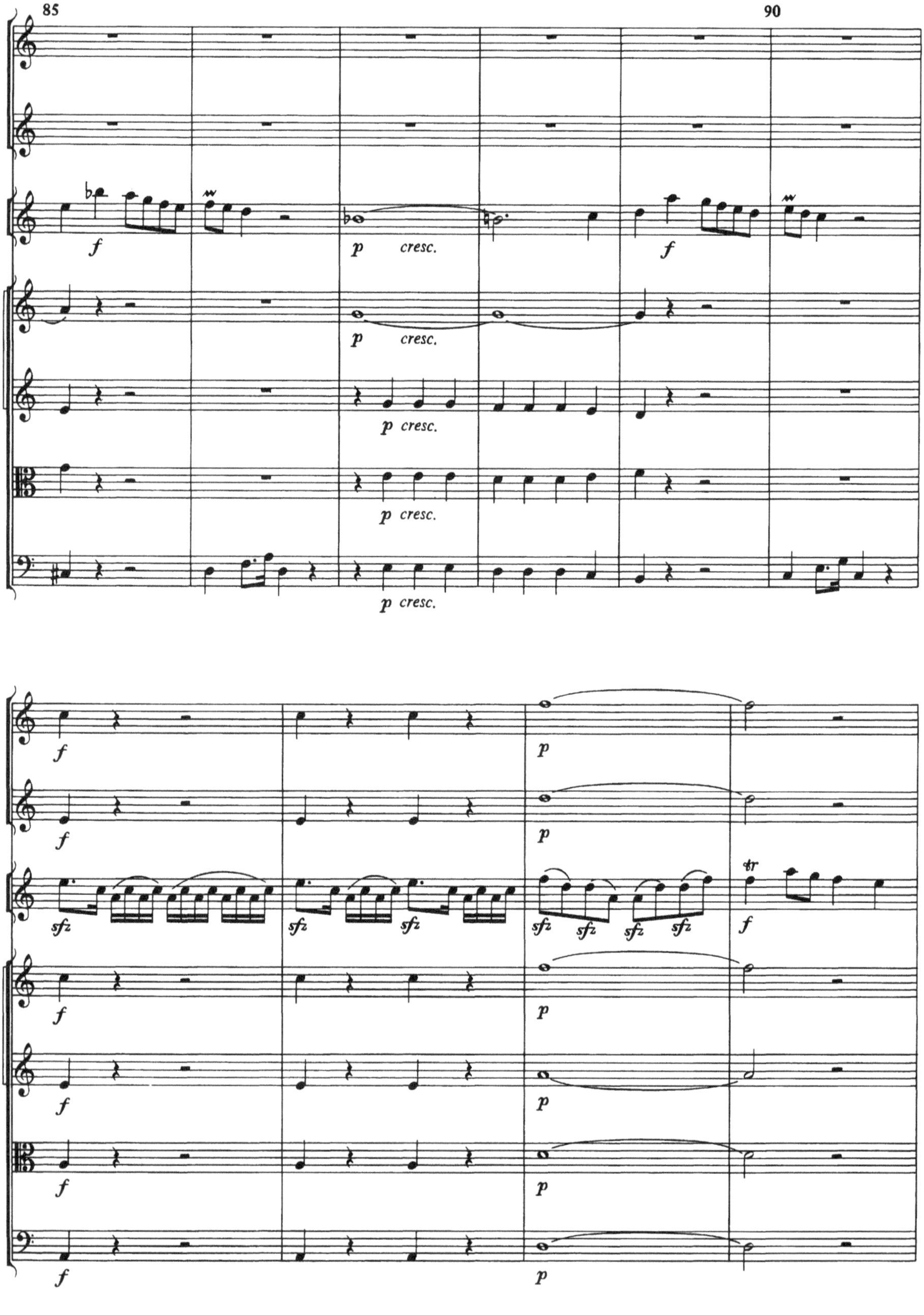
85
90
f
p cresc.
sfz
tr

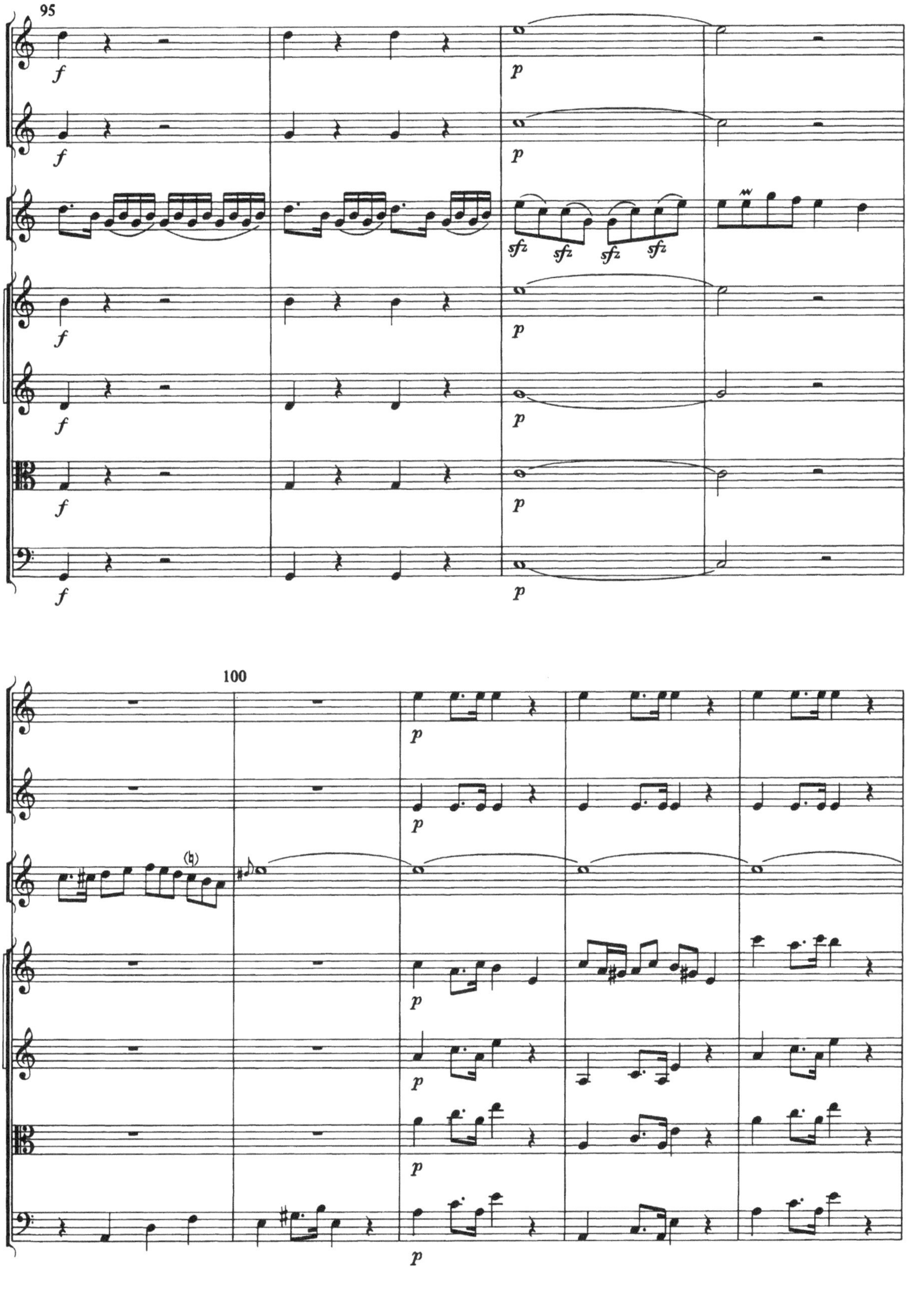
95
f
p
sfz
100
(♮)

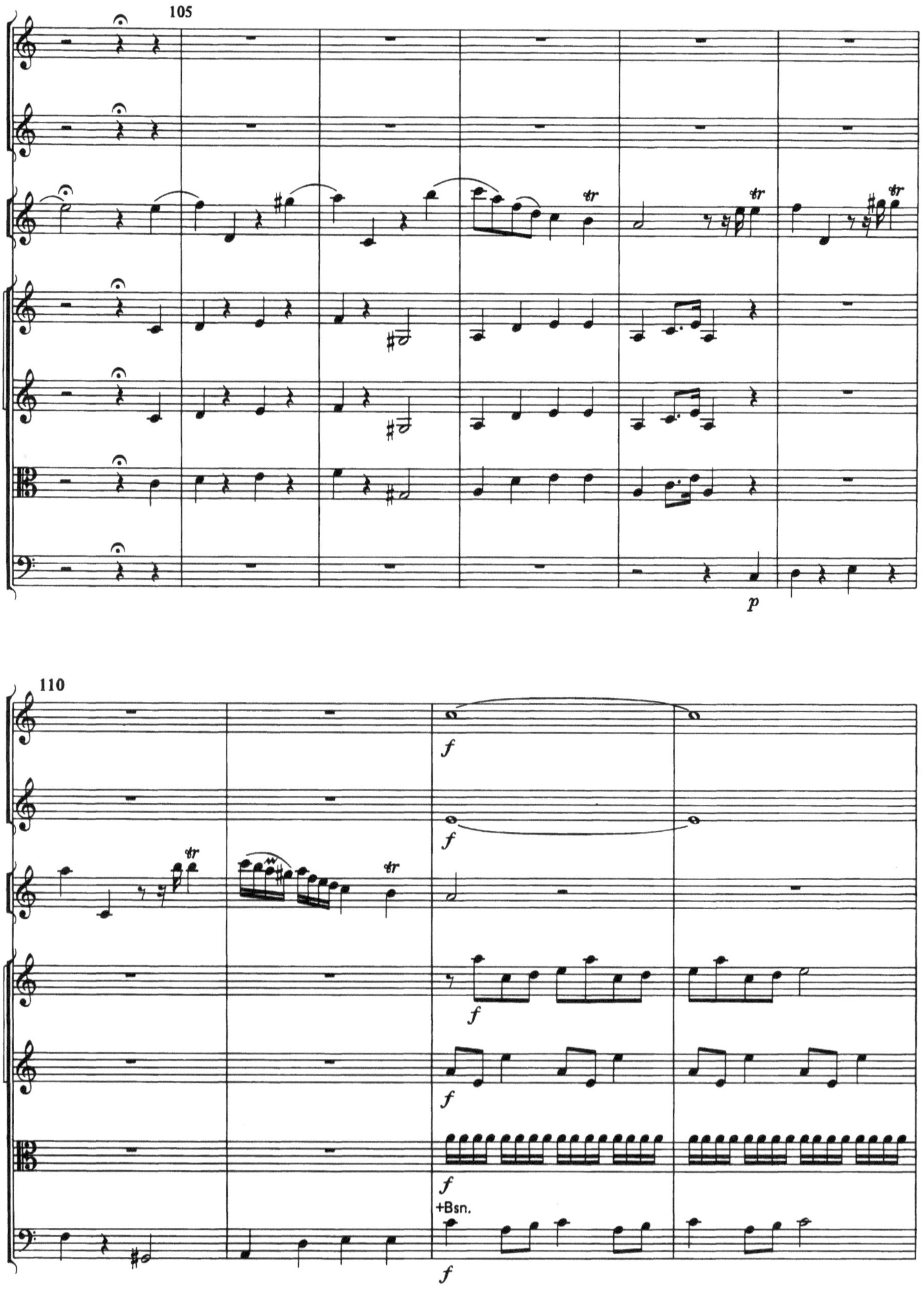
105
tr
p
110
tr
f
+Bsn.

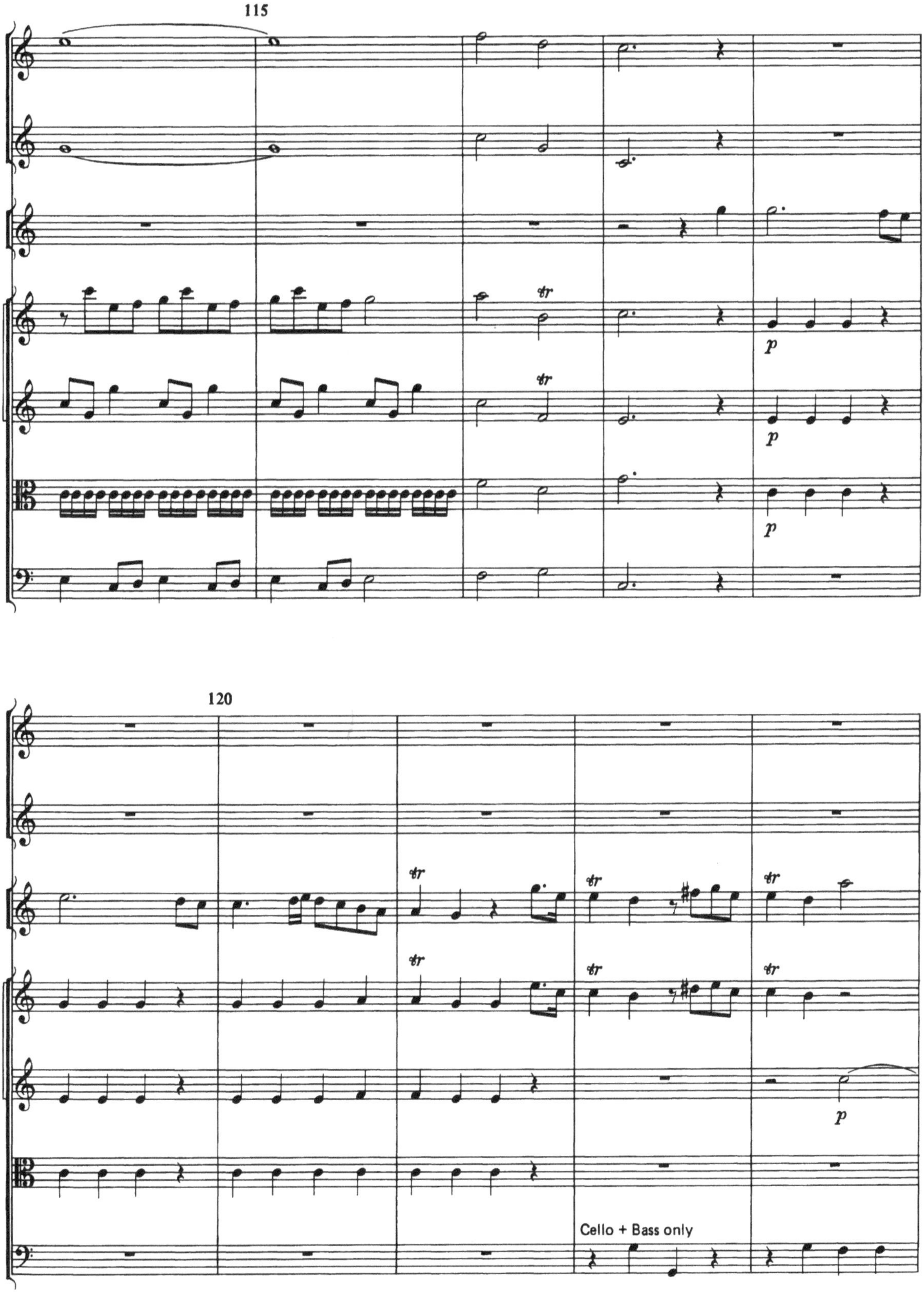
115
tr
p
120
Cello + Bass only

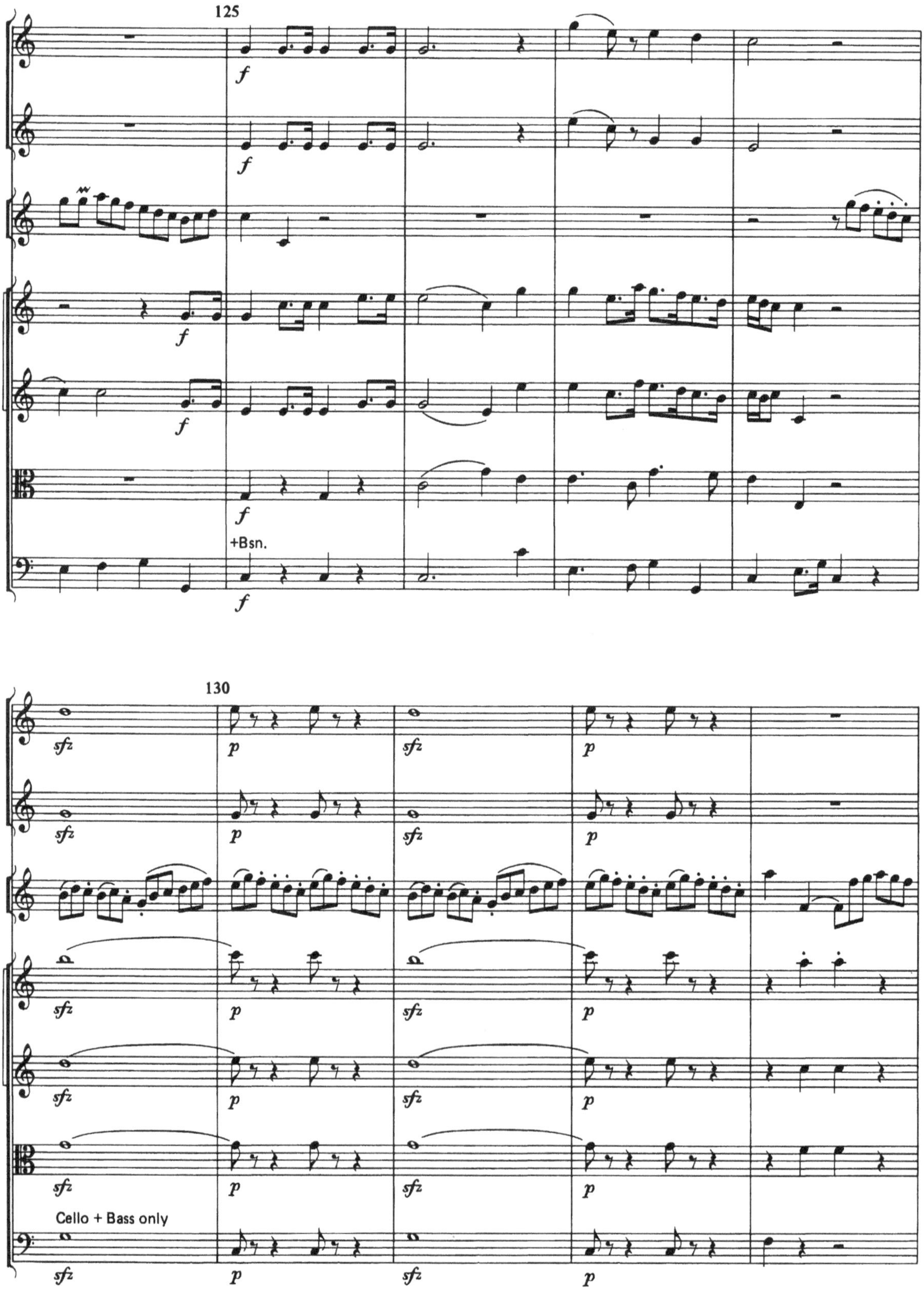
125
f
f
f
f
f
+Bsn.
f
130
sfz
p
sfz
p
Cello + Bass only

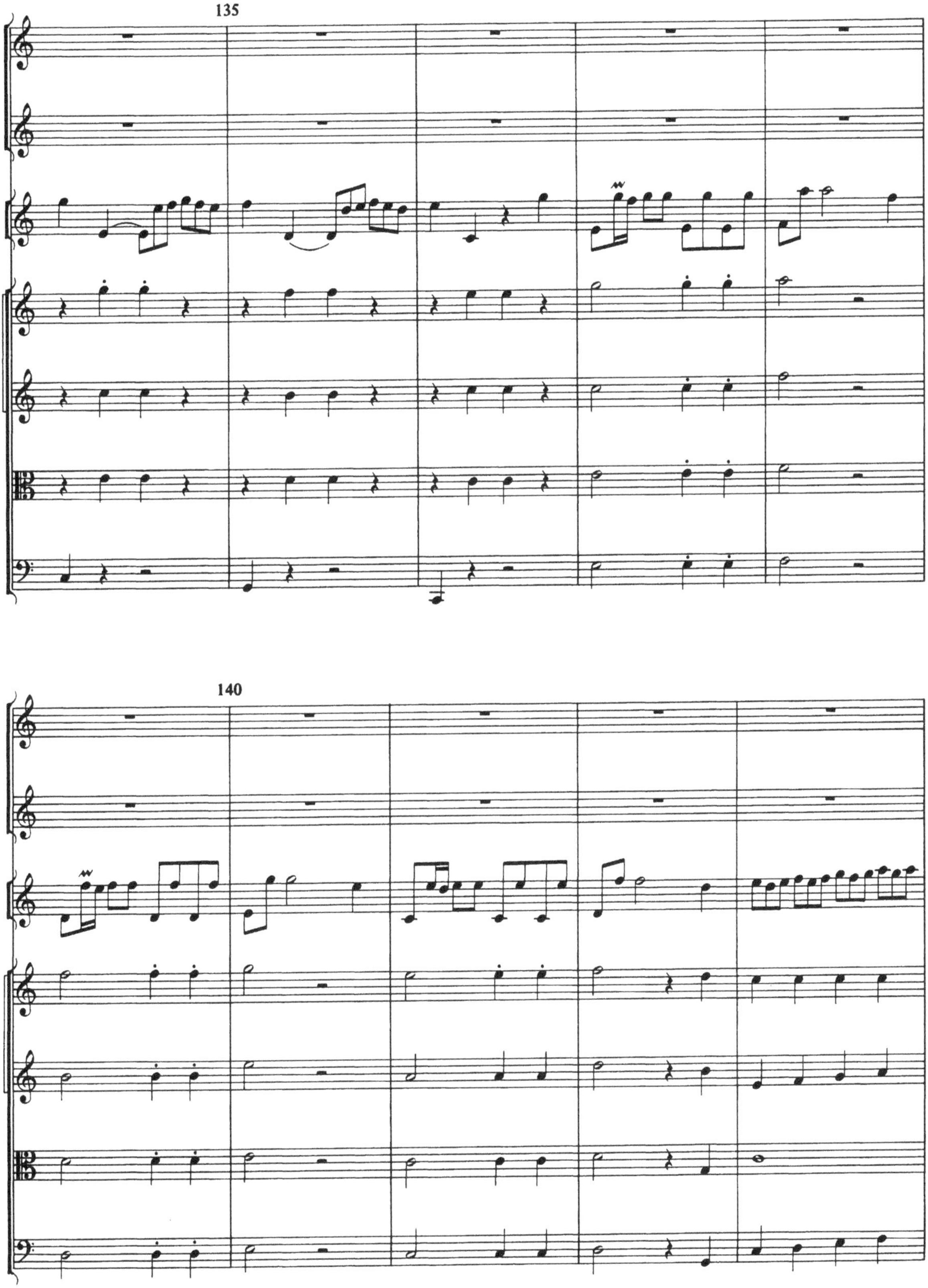
135
140

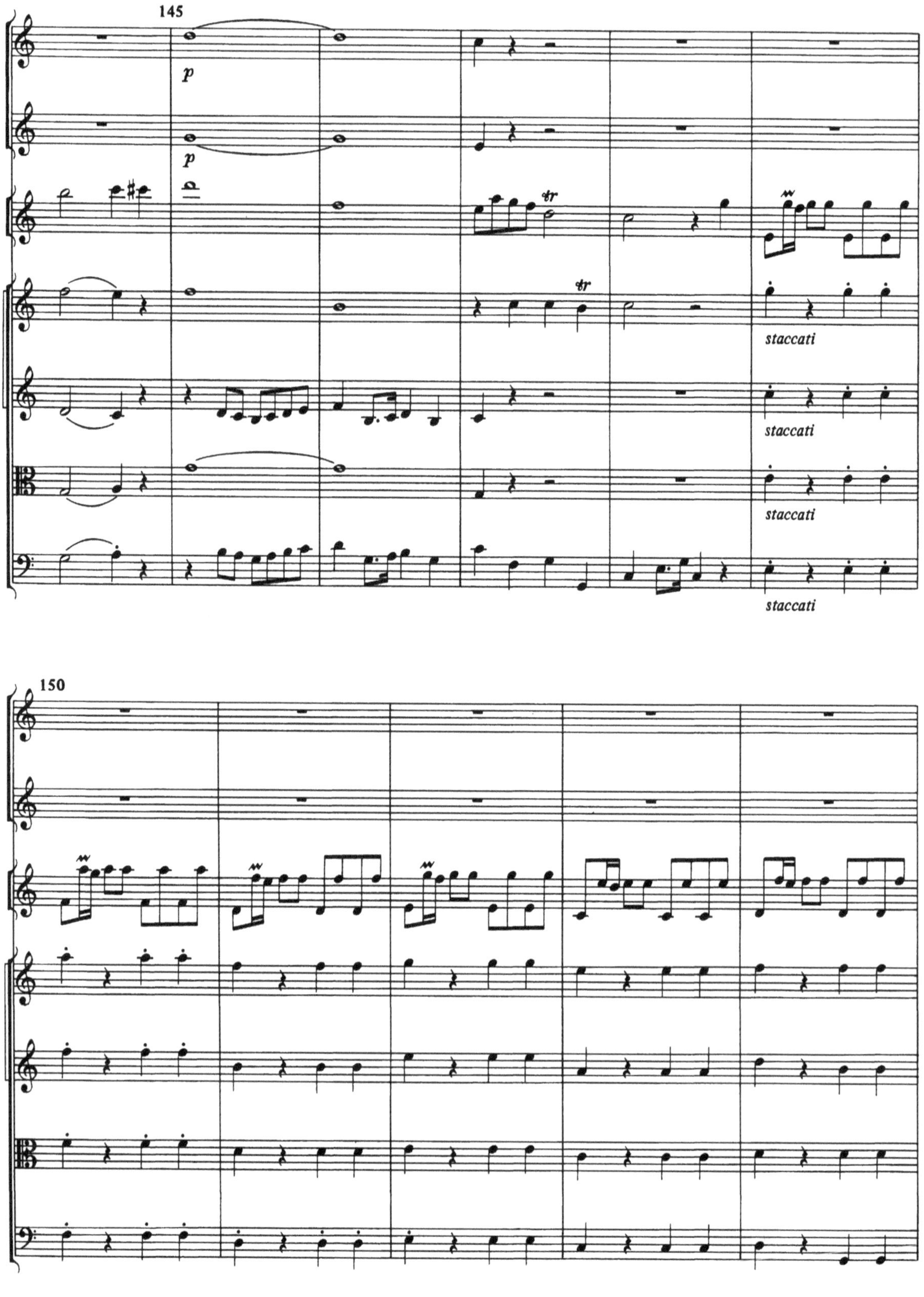
145
p
p
tr
tr
staccati
staccati
staccati
staccati
150

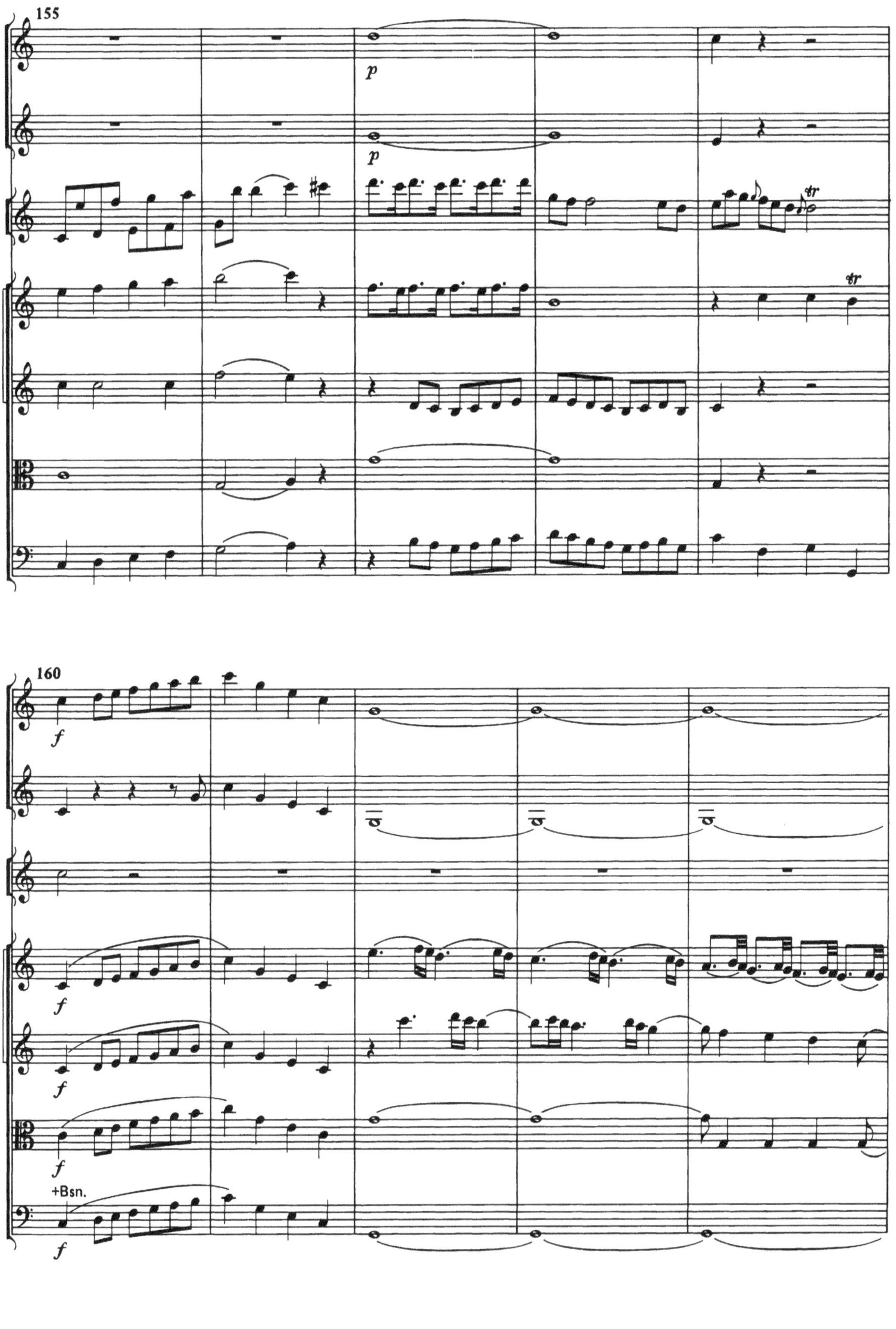
155
p
p
tr
tr
160
f
f
f
f
+Bsn.
f

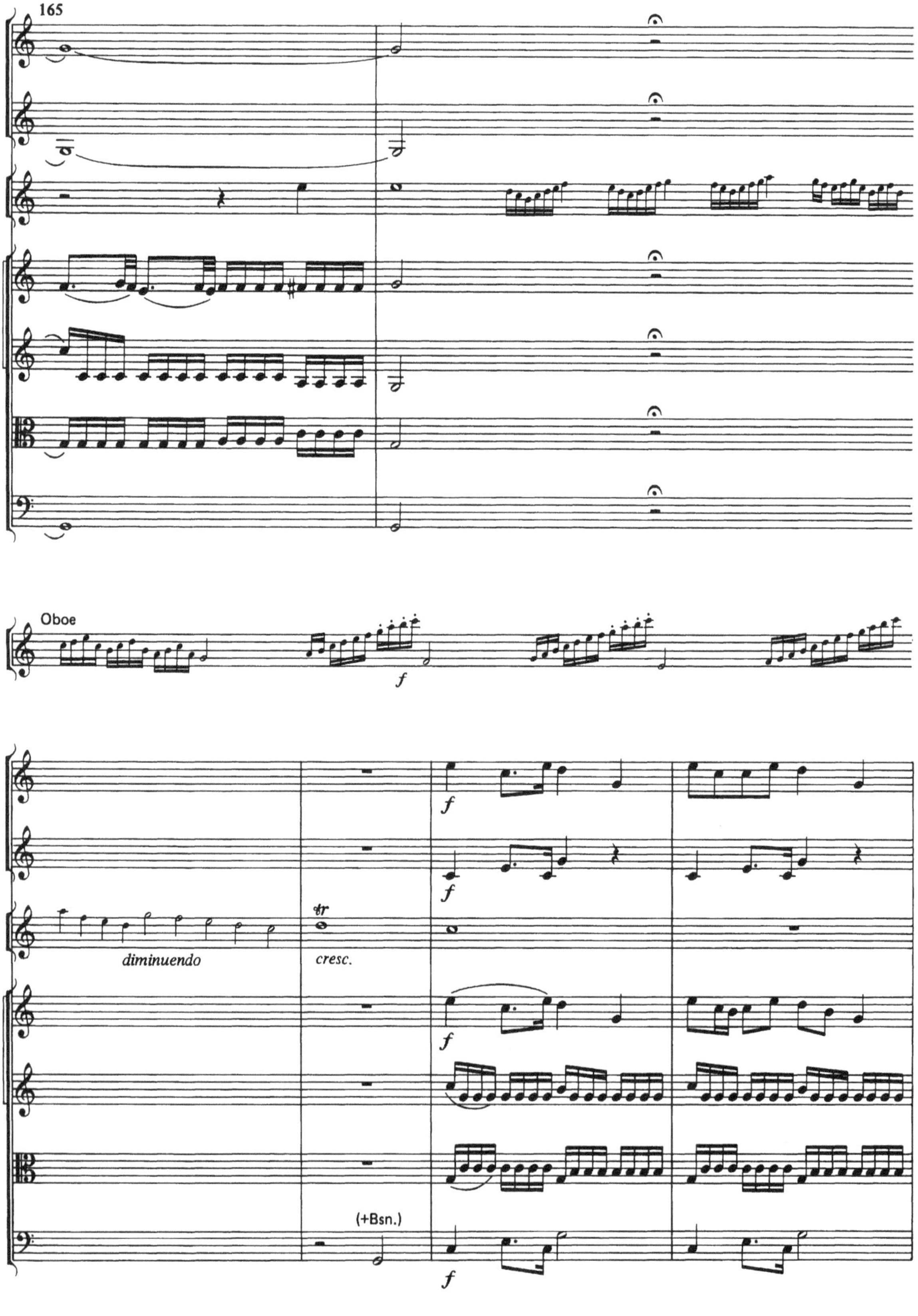
165
Oboe
f
diminuendo
cresc.
(+Bsn.)
f
f
f
f

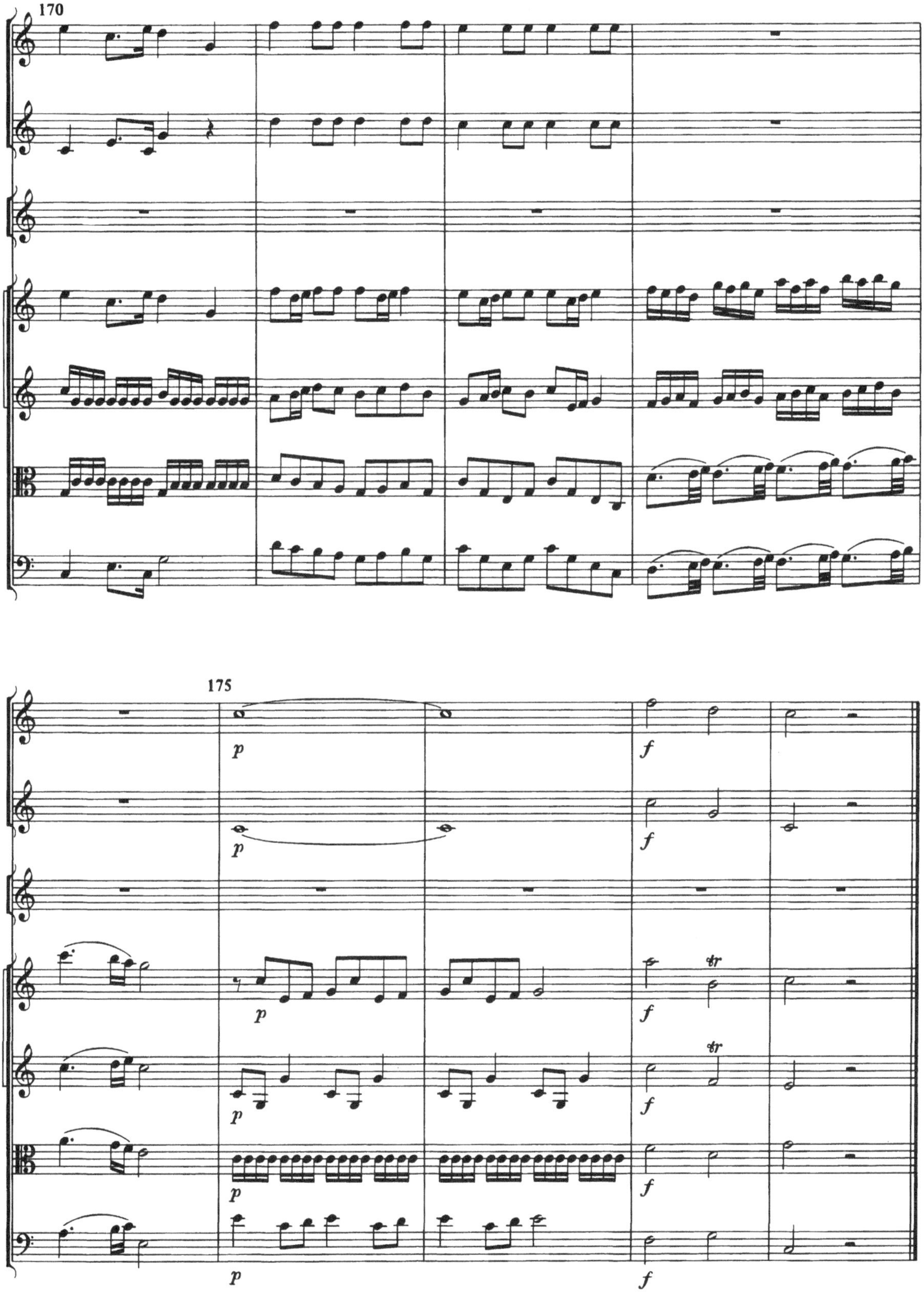
170
175

# II

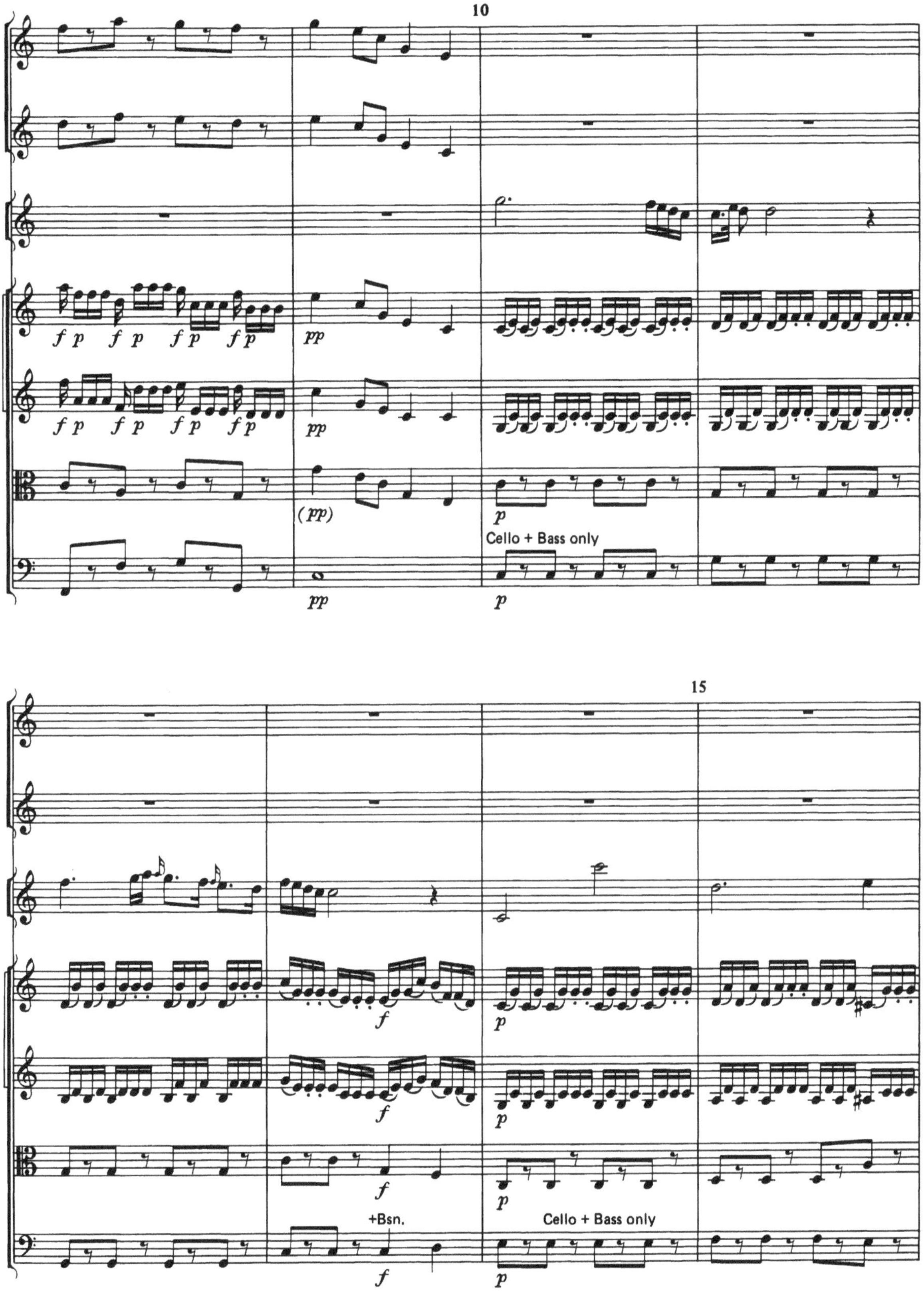
10
Cello + Bass only
15
+Bsn.
Cello + Bass only

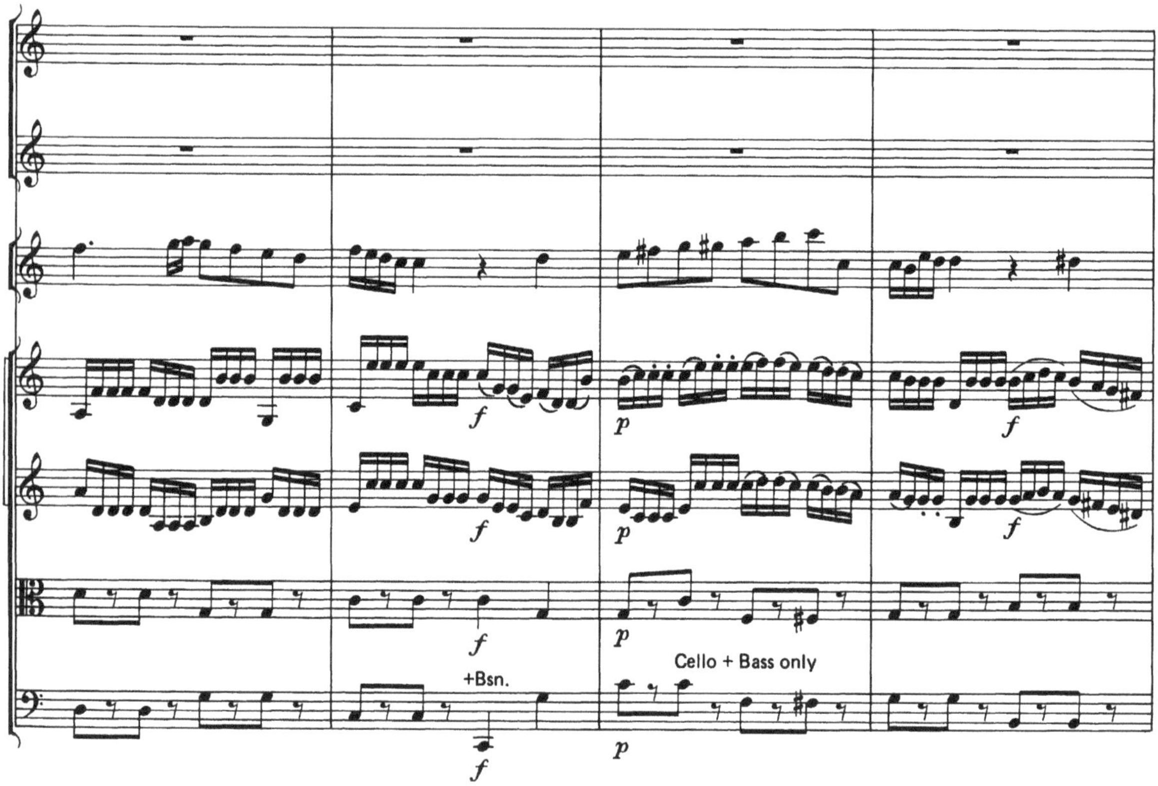
f
p
+Bsn.
Cello + Bass only

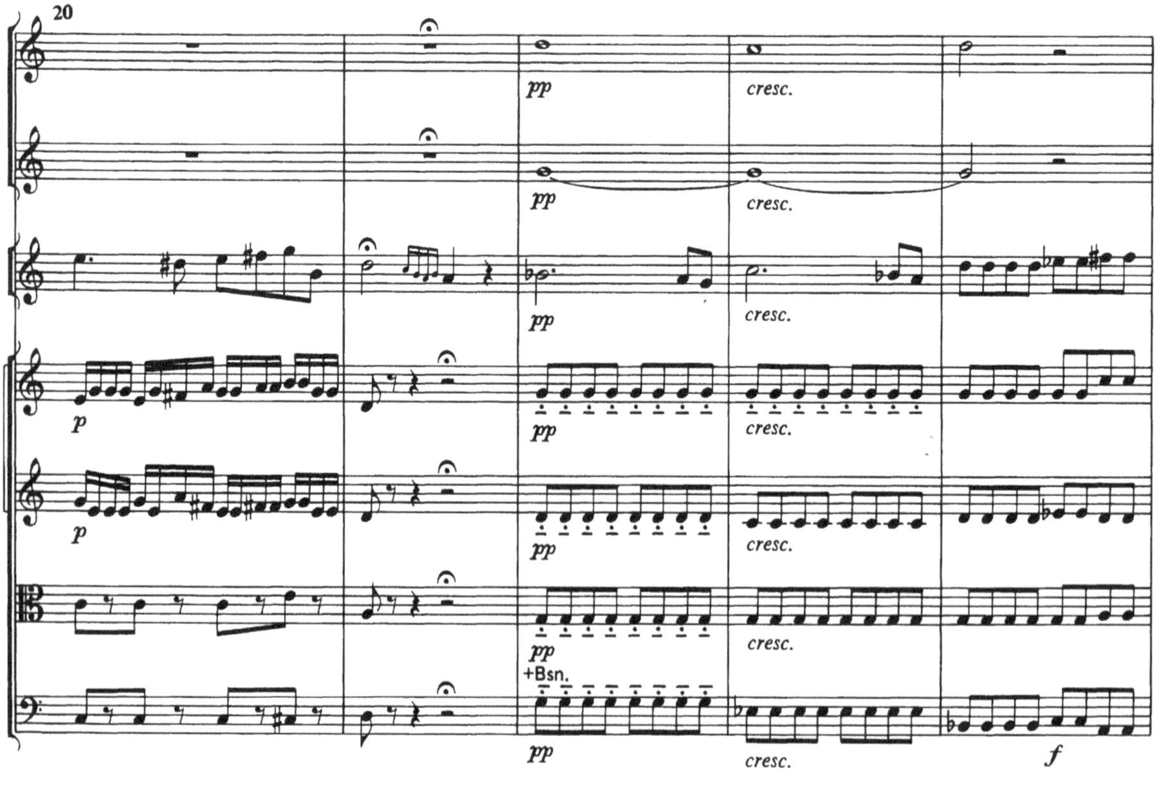
20
pp
cresc.
p
+Bsn.
f

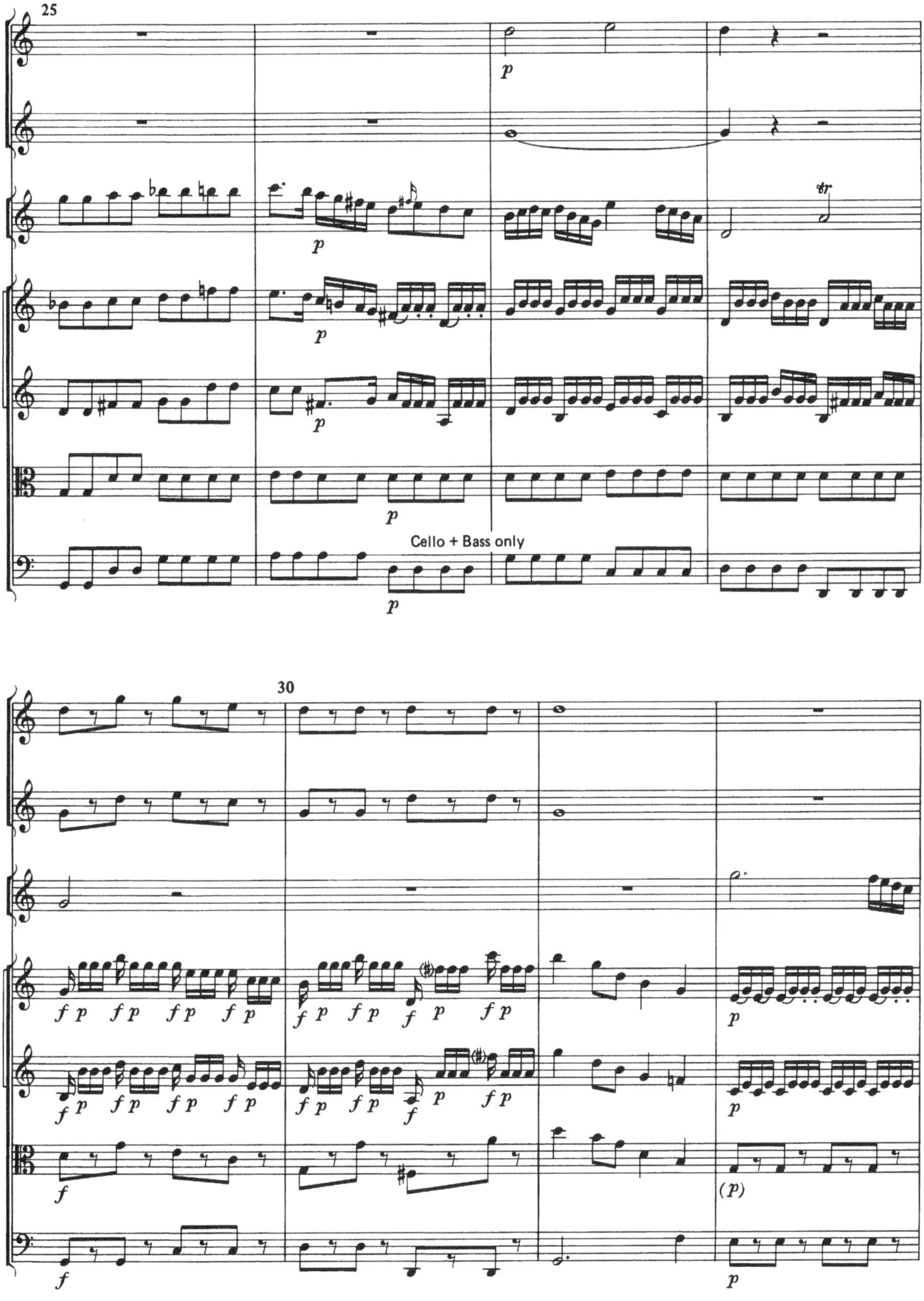
25
Cello + Bass only
30

35
f
p
+Bsn.
Cello + Bass only
+Bsn.
Cello + Bass only

40
cresc.
f
p
cresc.
(p)
+Bsn.
Cello + Bass only

p
cresc.
p
cresc.
p
cresc.
pp
cresc.
pp
cresc.
pp
cresc.
+Bsn.
pp
cresc.
45
Solo
p
Solo
p
tr
p
p
p
Cello + Bass only
p
tenuto
pp

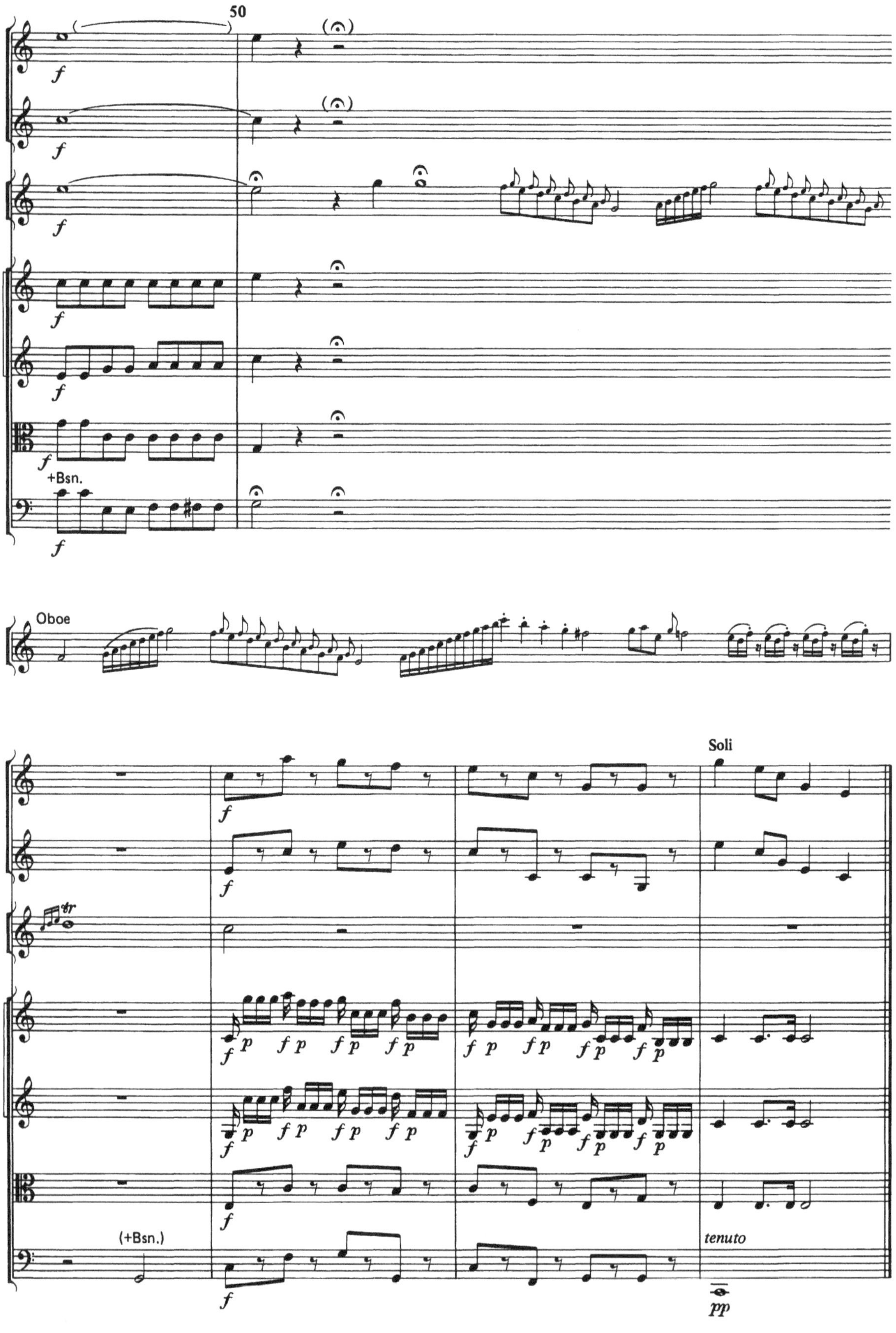
50
+Bsn.
Oboe
Soli
(+Bsn.)
tenuto

# III

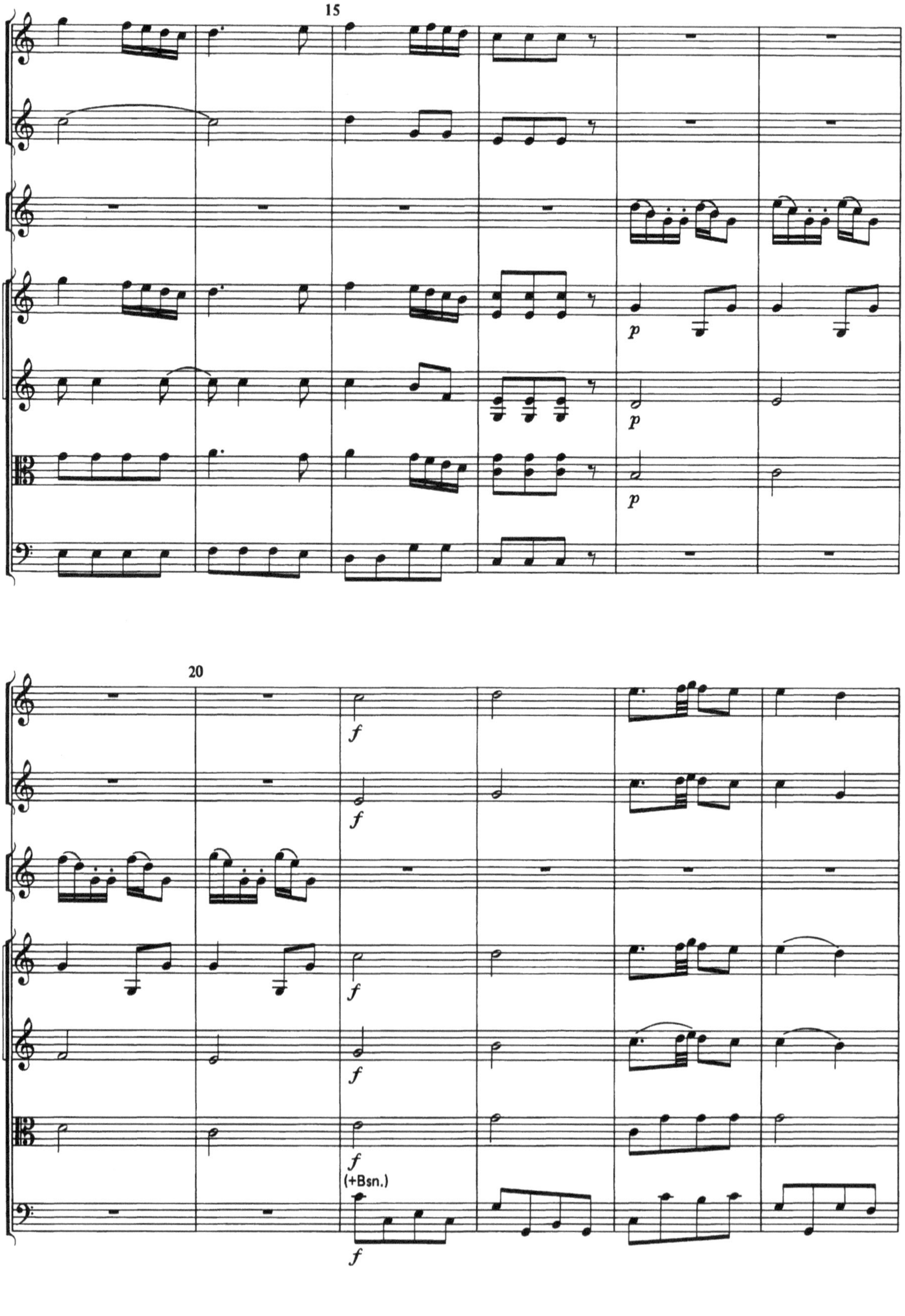
15
p
p
p
20
f
f
f
f
f
(+Bsn.)
f

Cello + Bass only

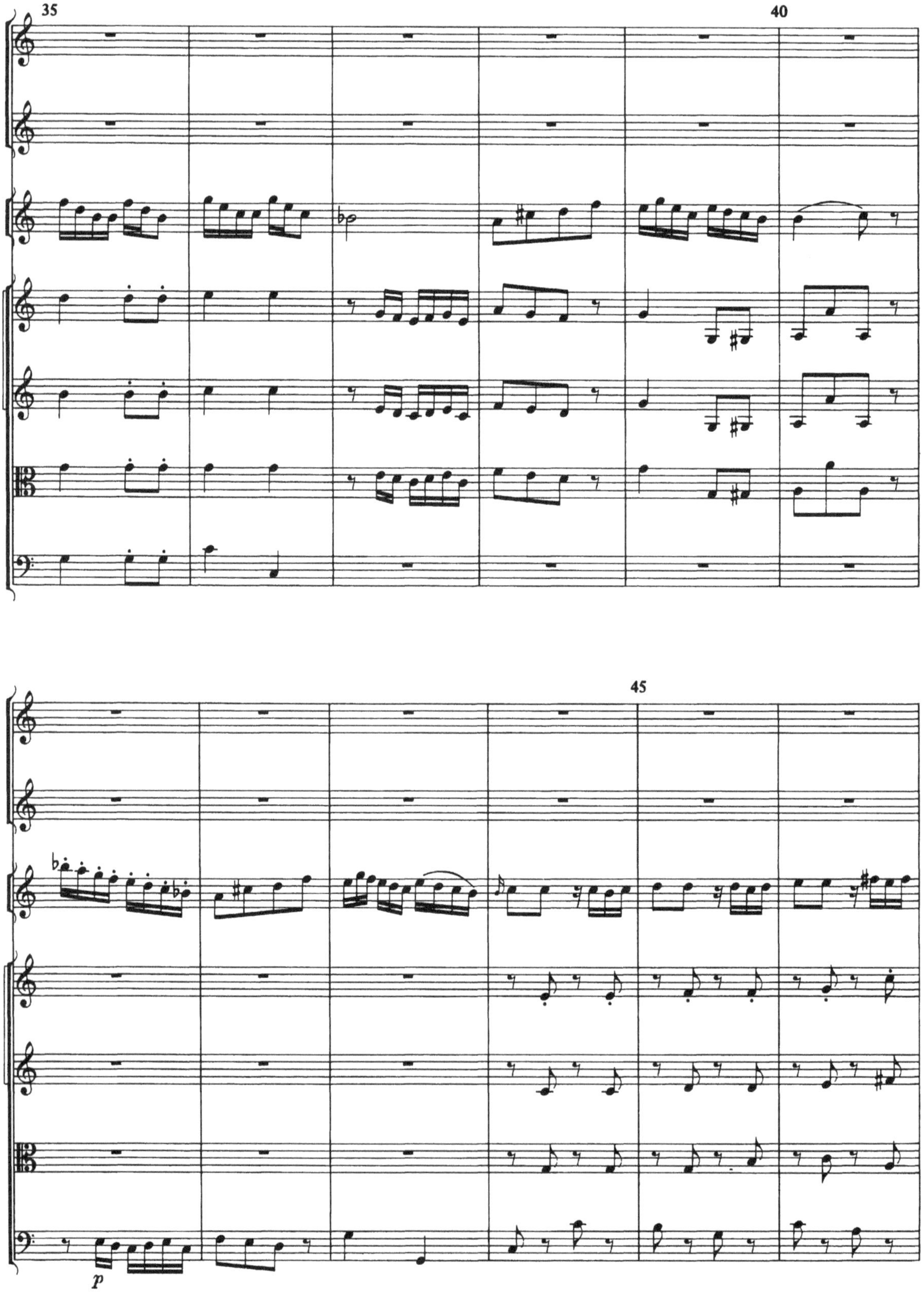
35
40
45
p

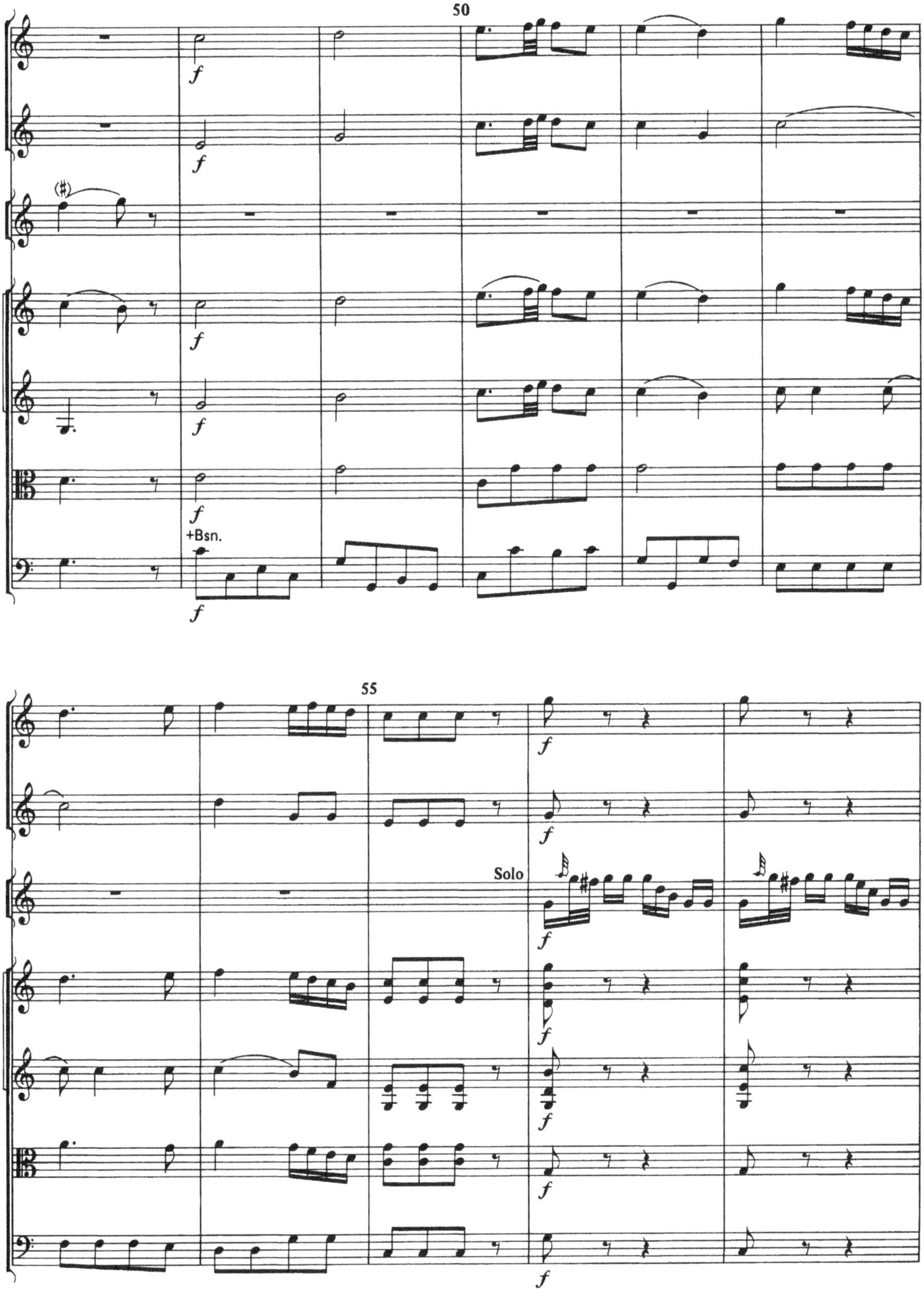
50
+Bsn.
55
Solo

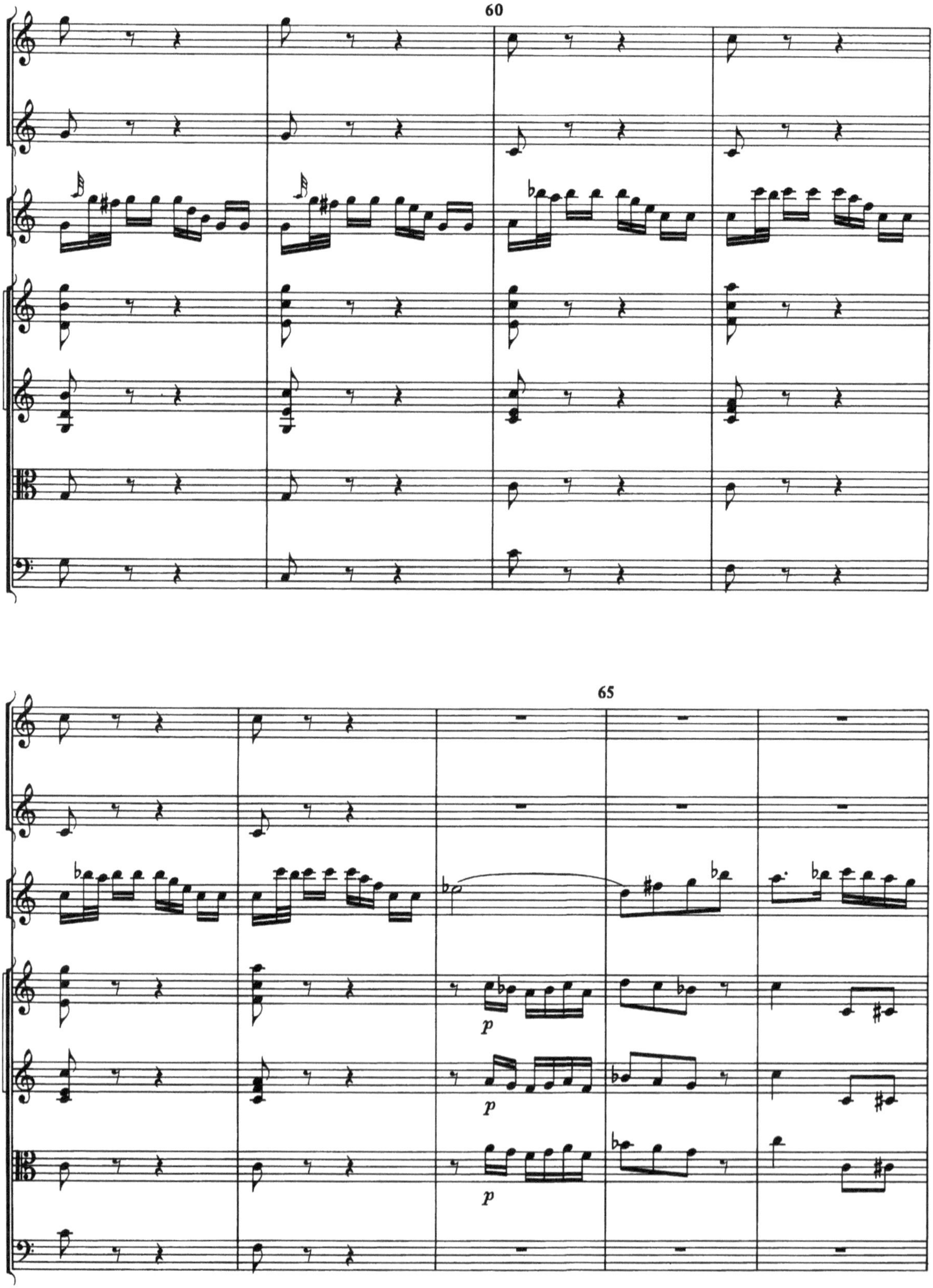
60
65
p
p
p

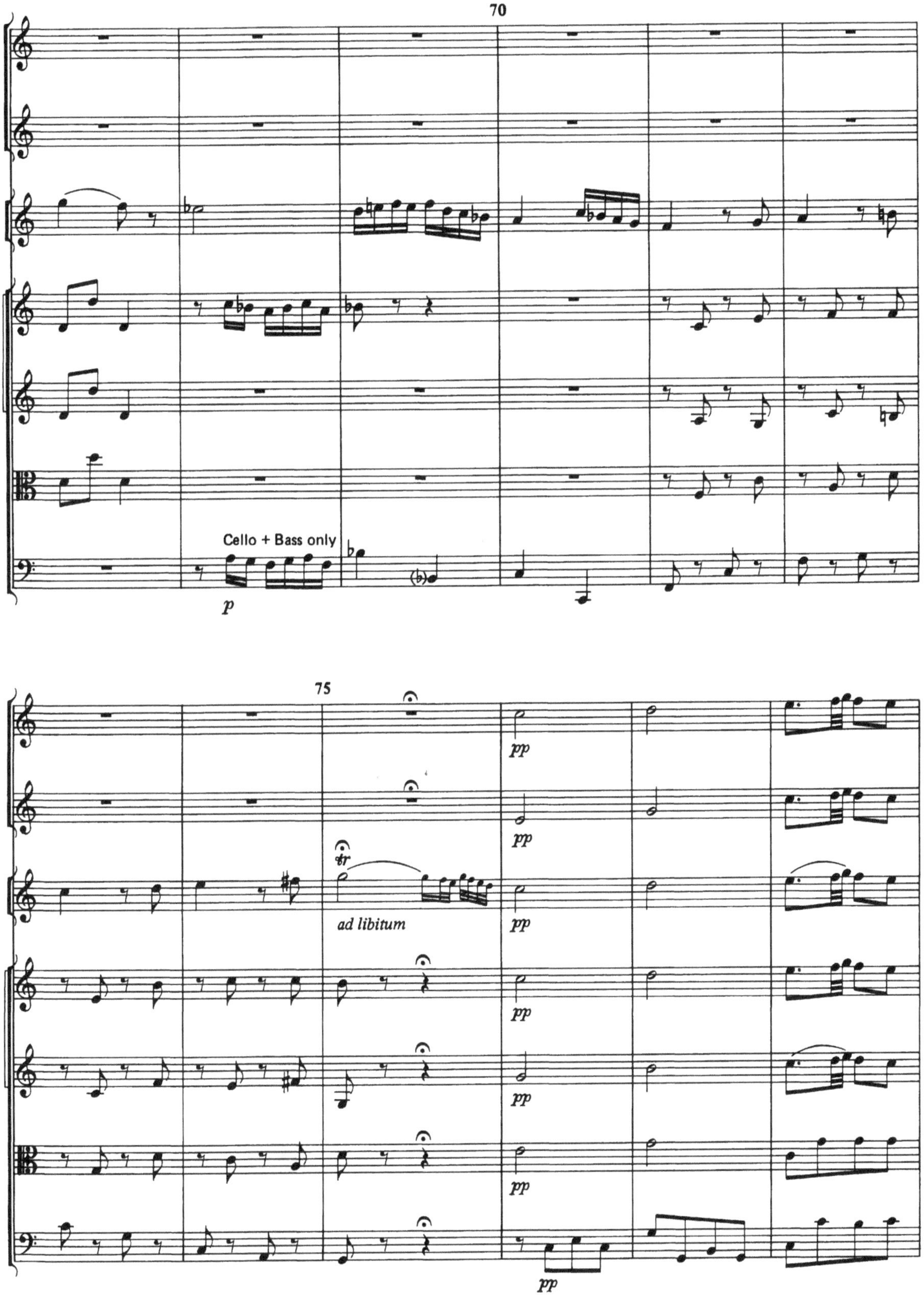
70
Cello + Bass only
p
(♭)
75
tr
ad libitum
pp

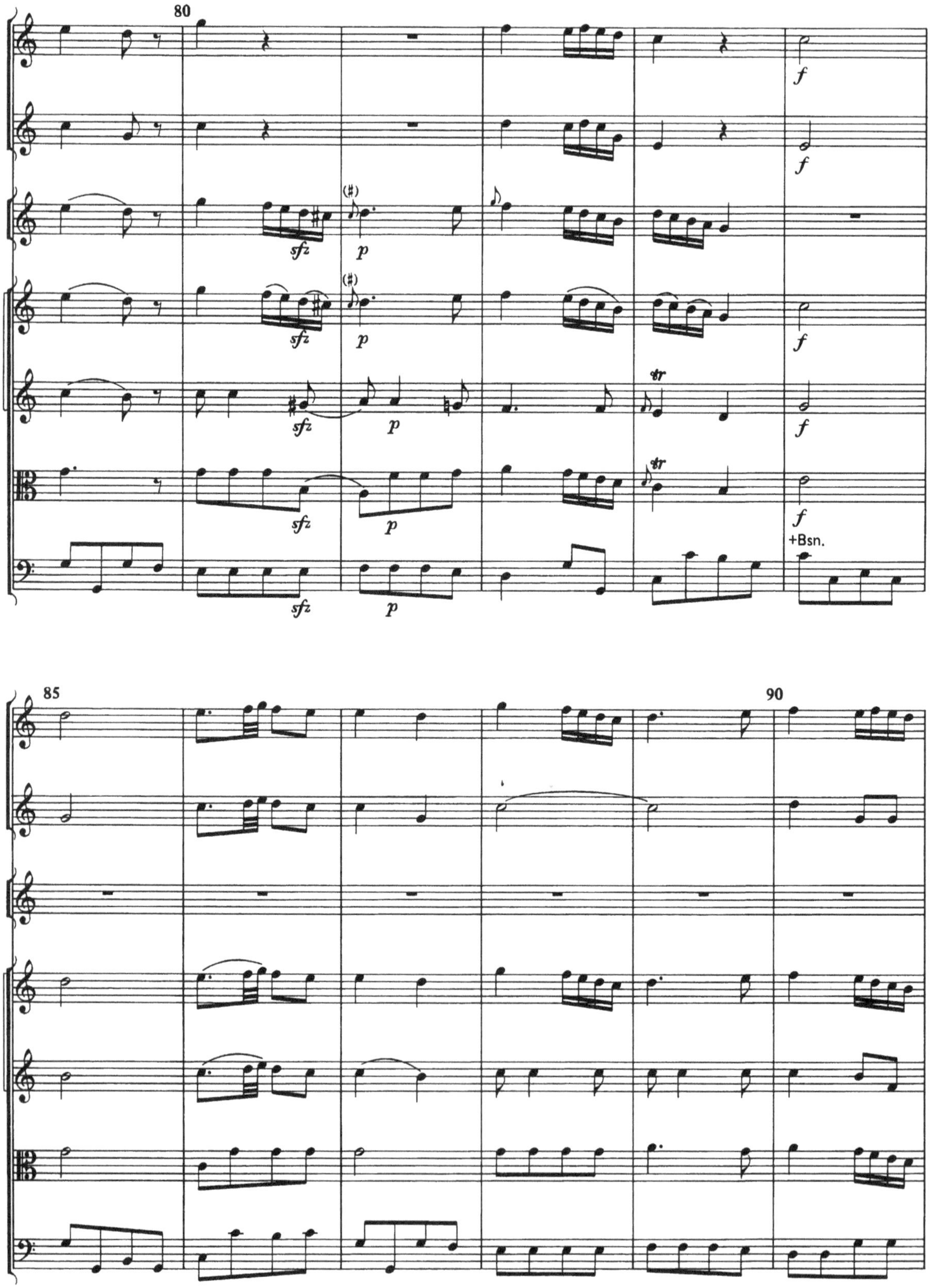
80
(♯)
sfz
p
tr
f
+Bsn.
85
90

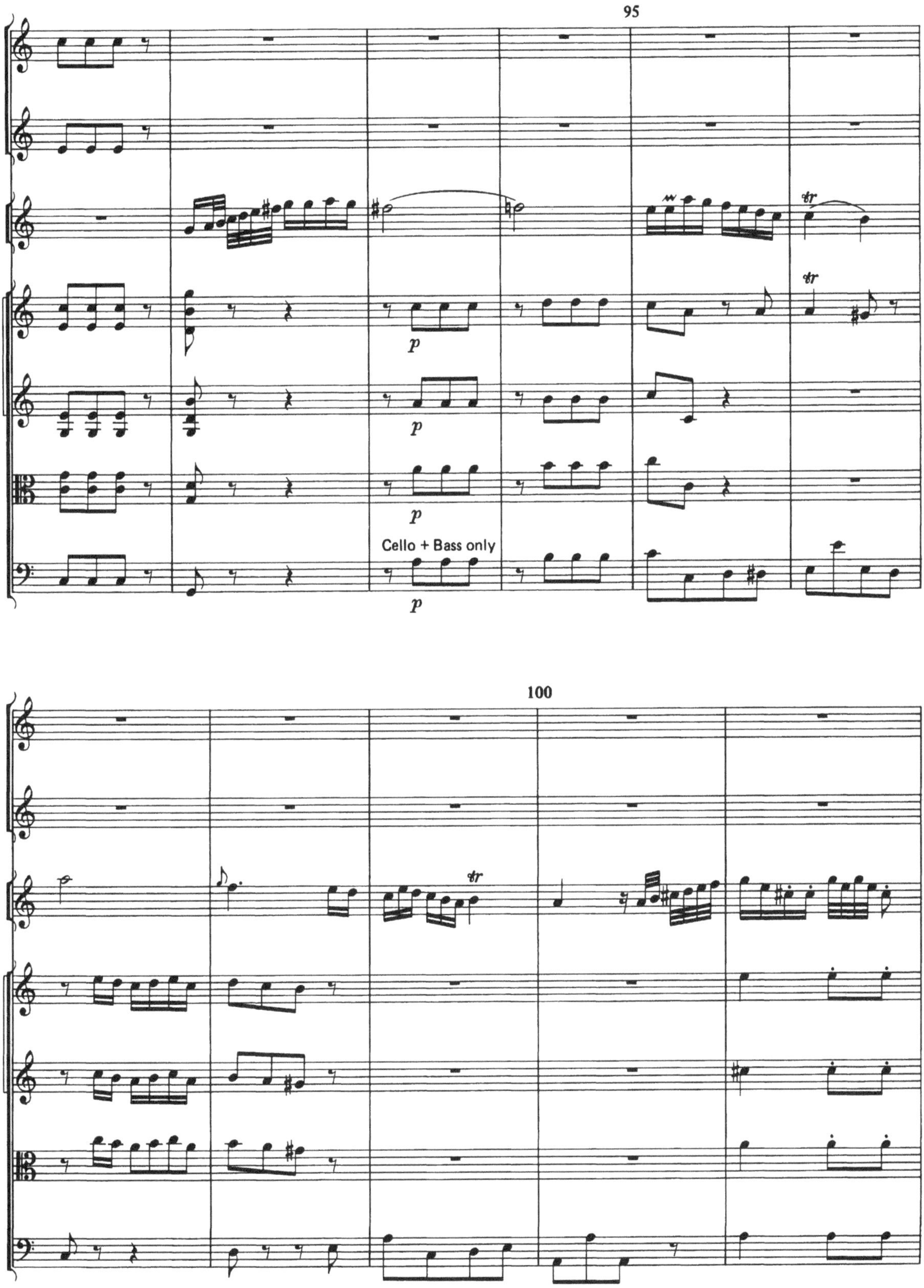
95
p
p
p
Cello + Bass only
p
100

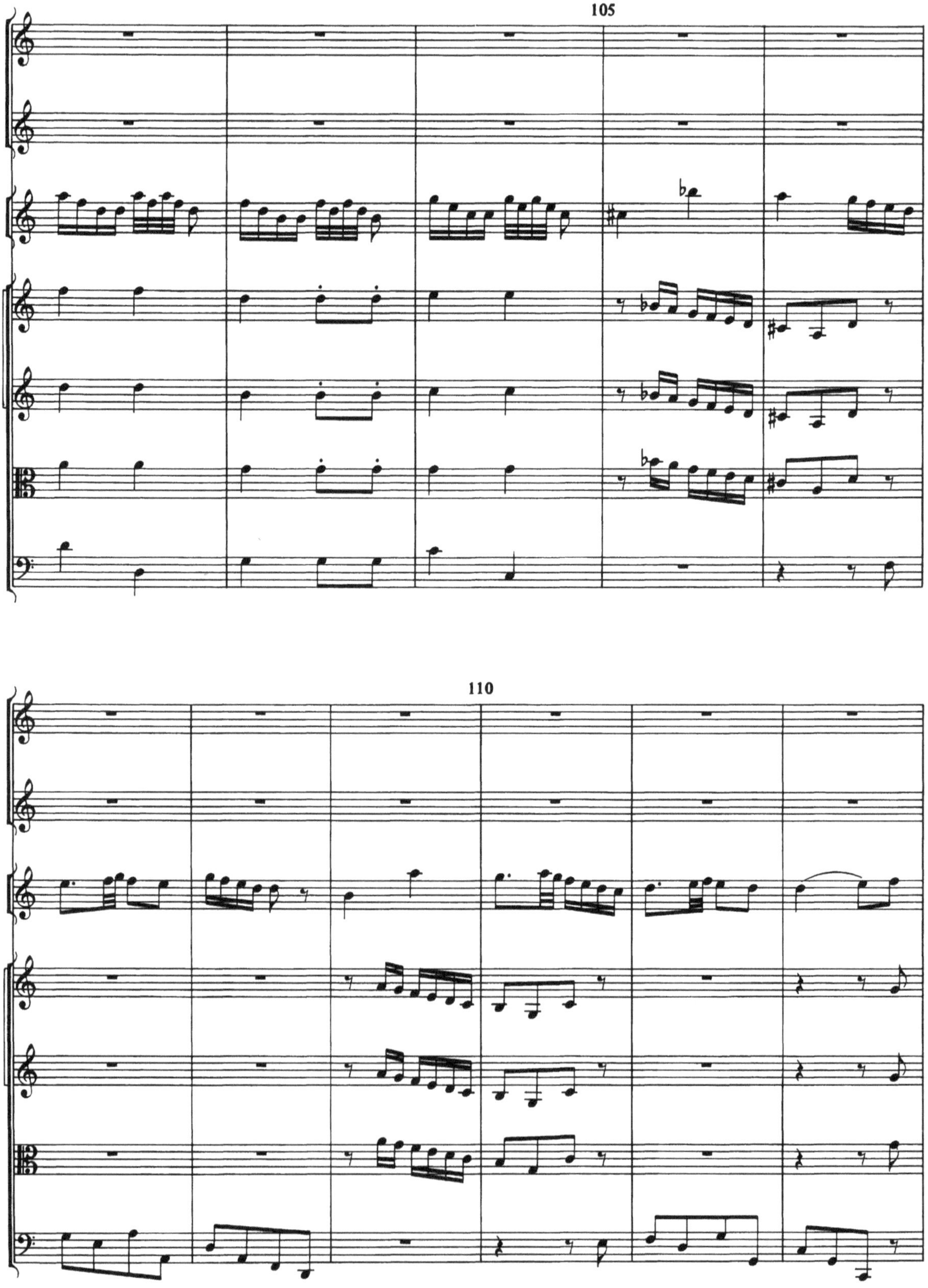
105
110

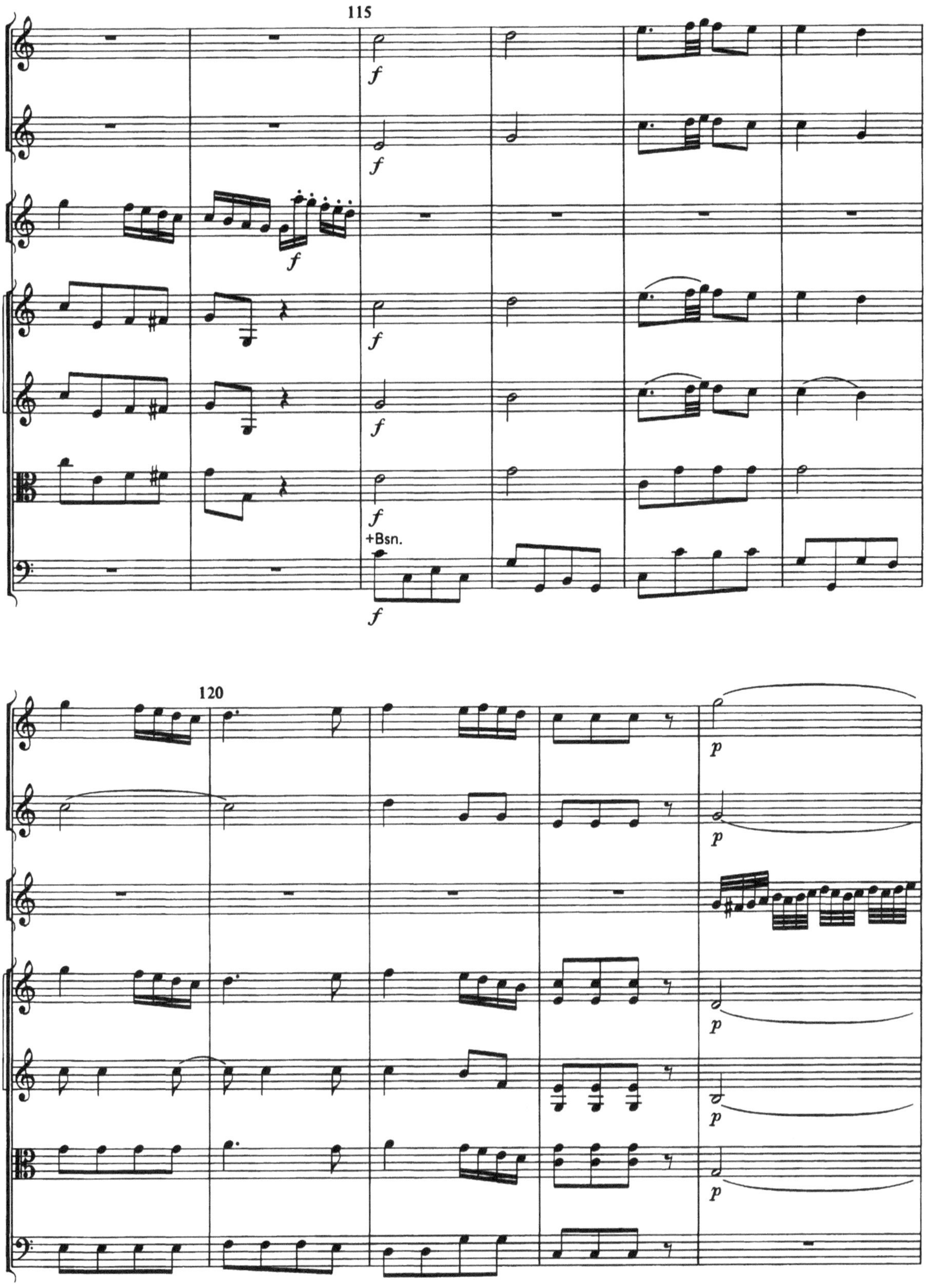
115
+Bsn.
120

125

130

Cello + Bass only

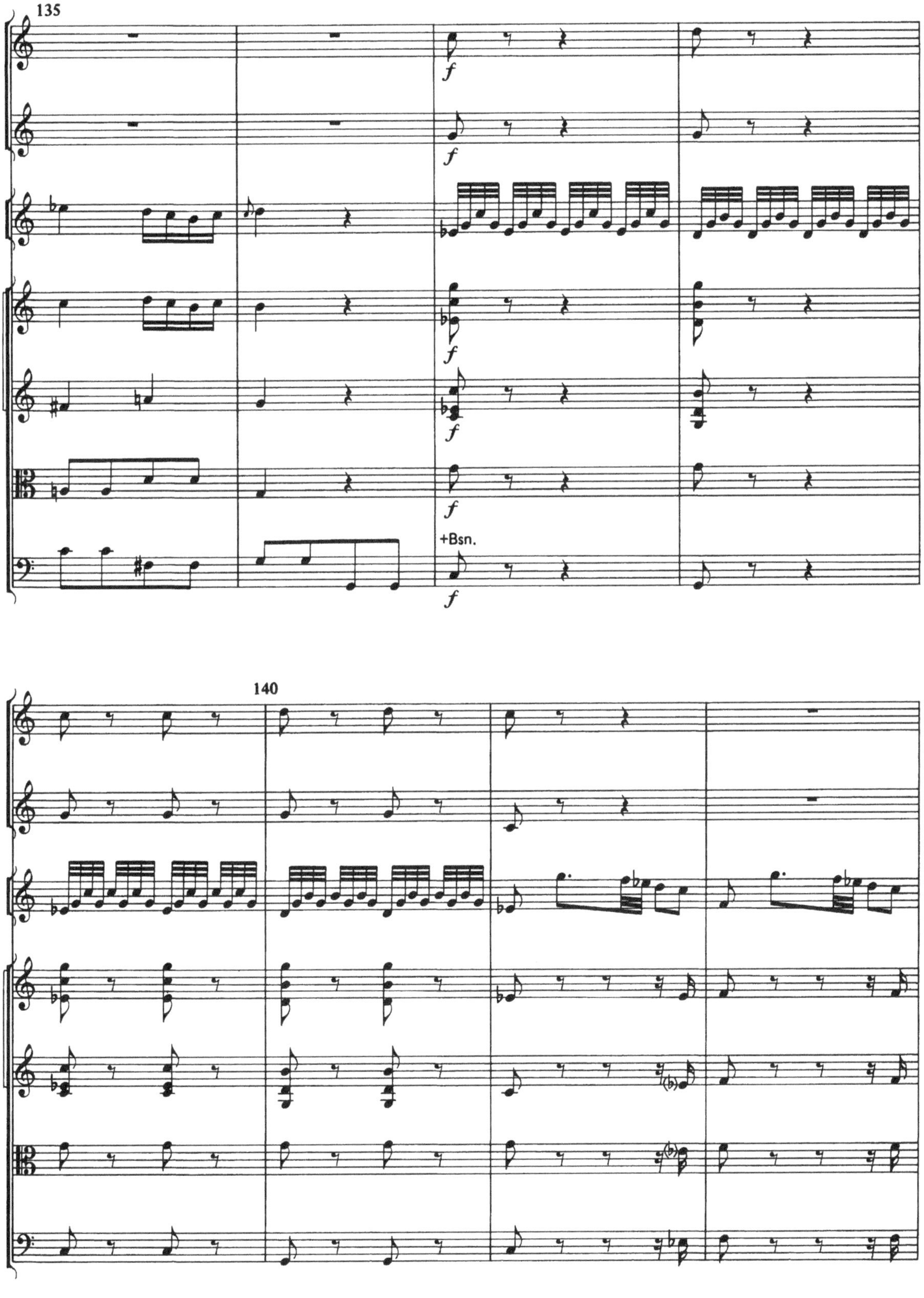
135
f
+Bsn.
140

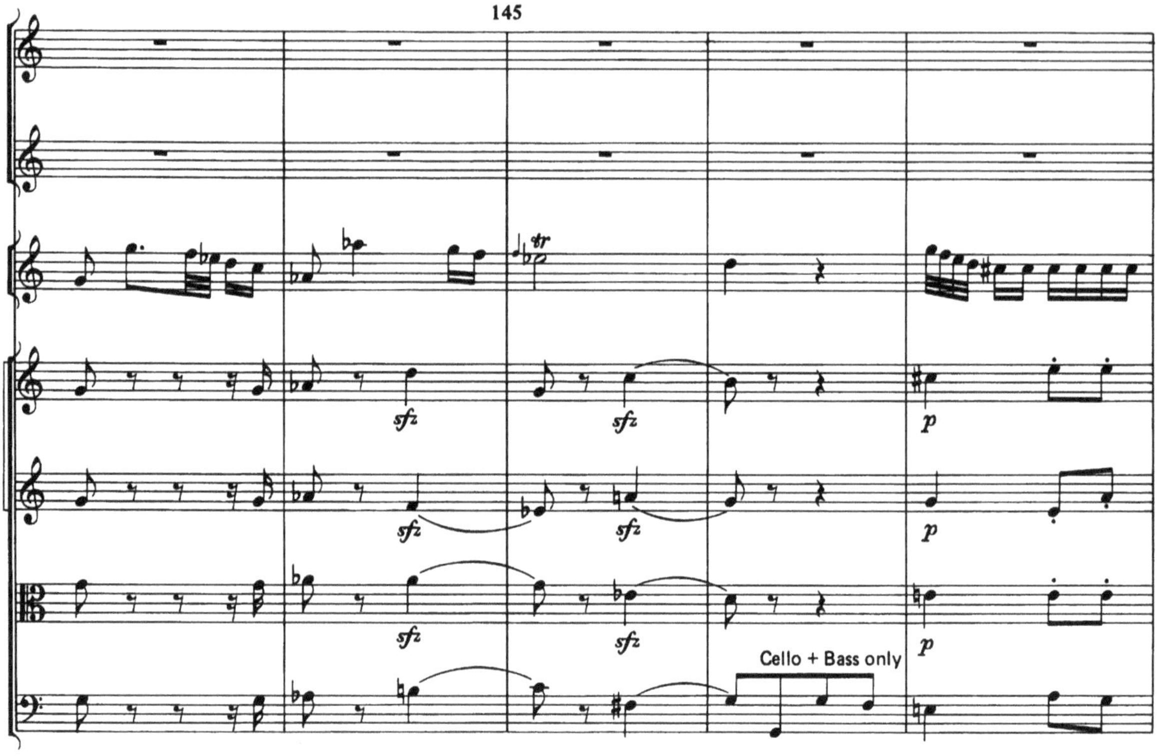
145
sfz
p
Cello + Bass only

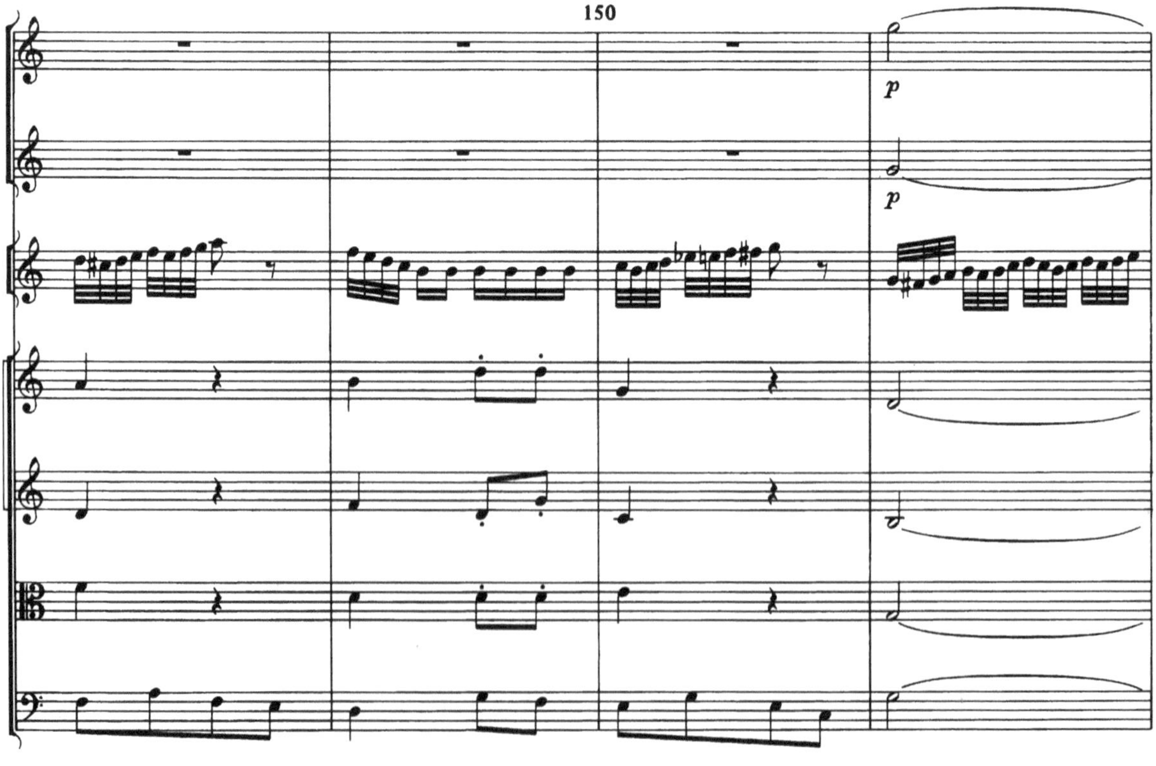
150
p

155
cresc.
cresc.
cresc.
cresc.
cresc.
cresc.
cresc.
160
f
f
f
f
f
+Bsn.
f

42

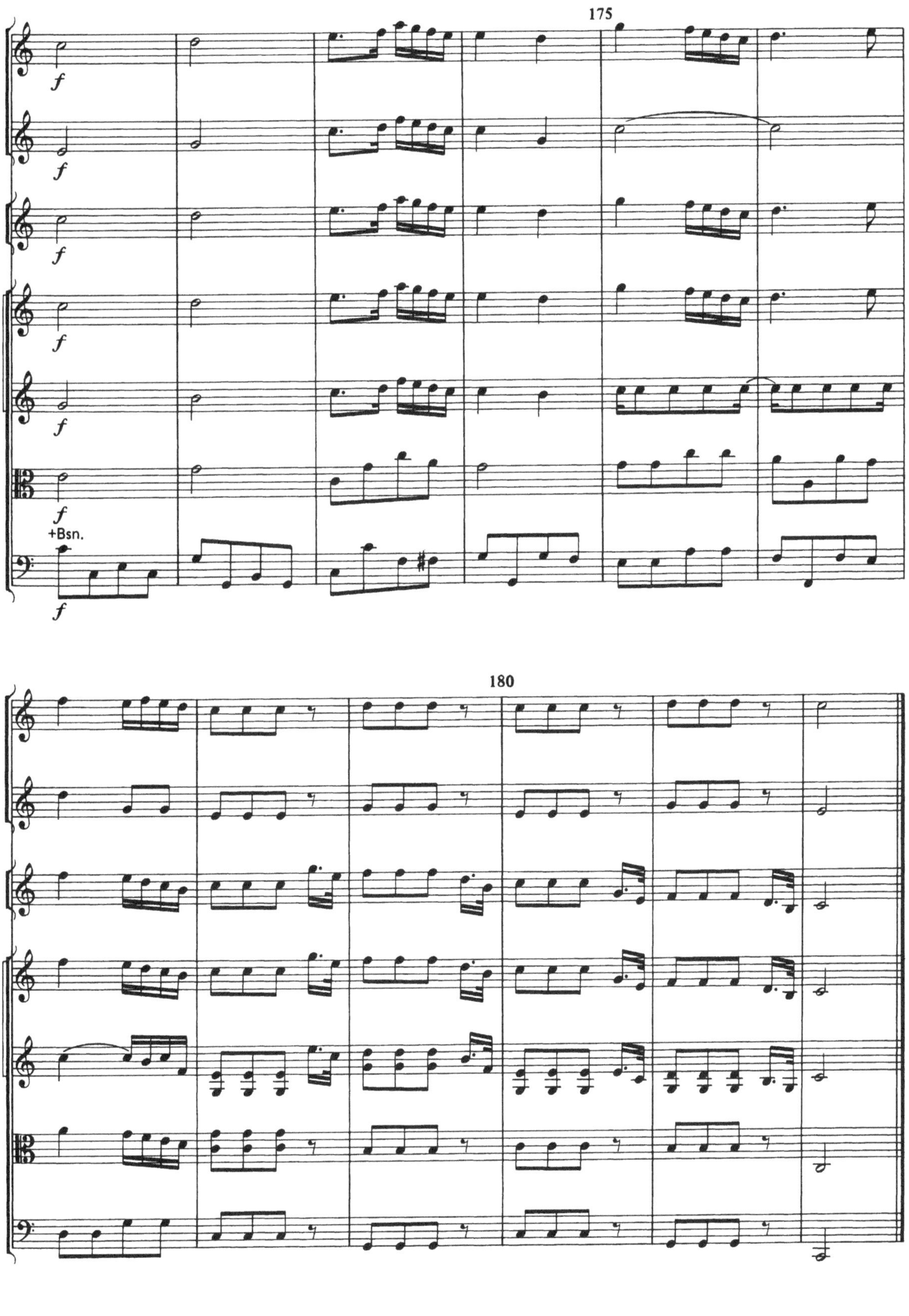
175
f
f
f
f
f
f
+Bsn.
f
180

# CONCERTO NO. 3 IN C

William Herschel

## I

1. See critical commentary for explanation of "Tutti" Oboe sections.
2. "G" in MS, Violin I, measure 3, fourth note.

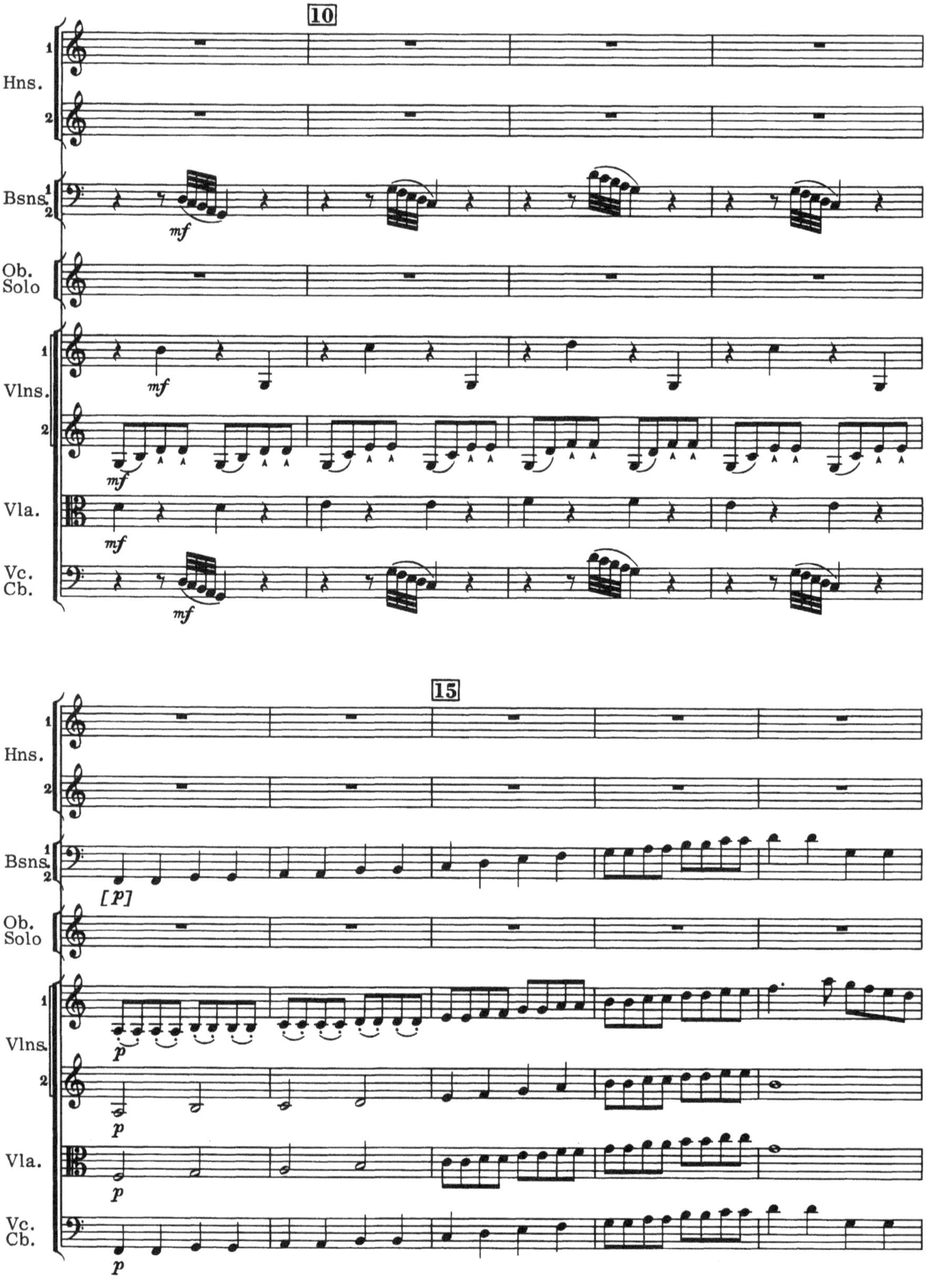
10
Hns. 1 2
Bsns. 1 2
Ob. Solo
Vlns. 1 2
Vla.
Vc. Cb.
mf
15
[p]
p

3. MS here designates 16 measures rest in Oboe part. Editor has used 17 measures.

4

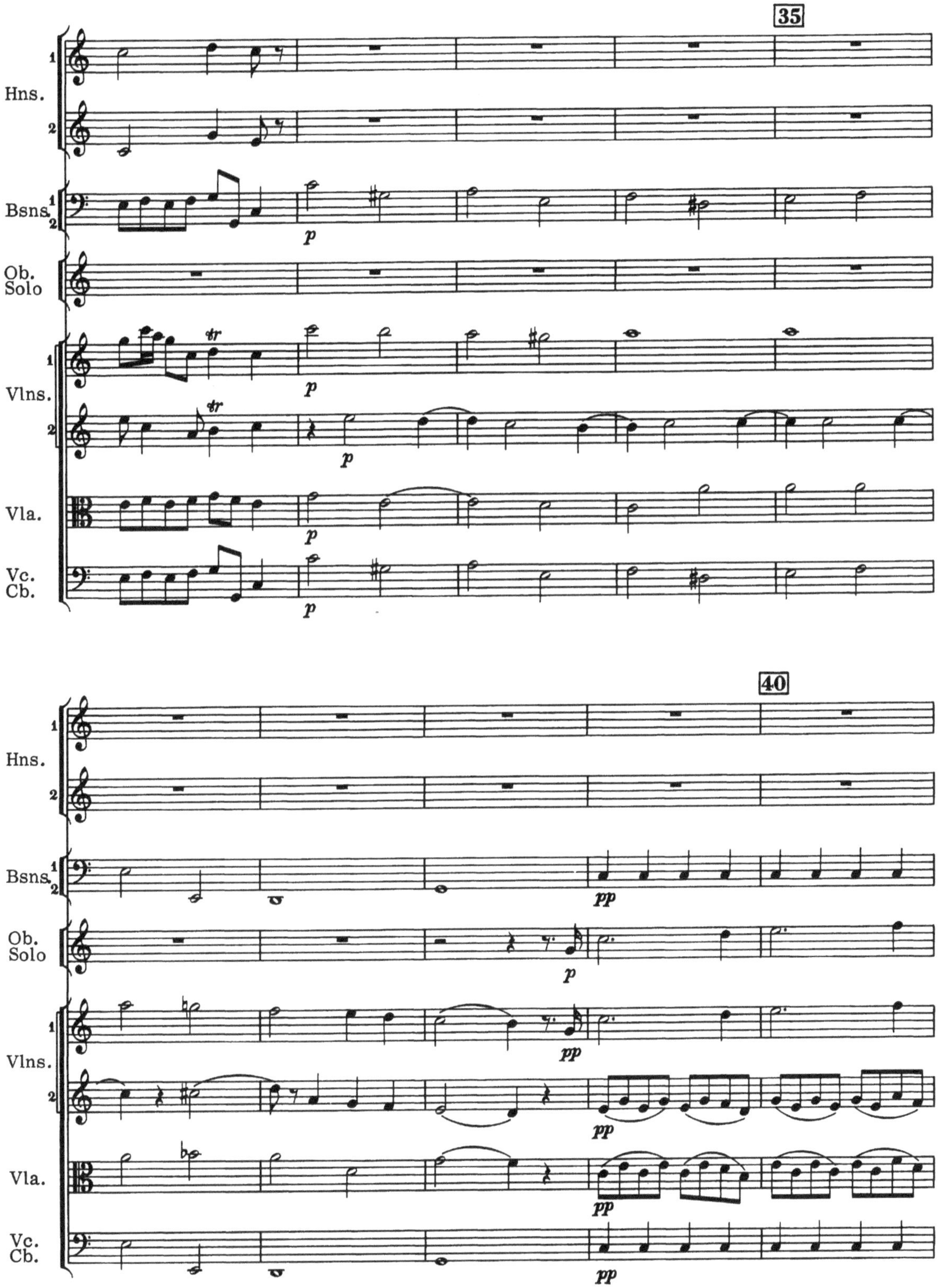
35
Hns.
1
2
Bsns.
1
2
Ob.
Solo
Vlns.
1
2
Vla.
Vc.
Cb.
p
tr
40
pp

*4.* MS here designates 4 measures rest in Oboe part. Editor has used 3 measures.

*5.* MS measure 43,  MS measure 43,  *6.* MS measure 45,
Violin II obligato part:  Violin II part:  first beat:

50
Hns.
Bsns.
Ob. Solo
Solo
[3]
Vlns.
Solo
p
Vla.
Solo
p
Vc. Cb.
Cello Solo
p
55
Hns.
Bsns.
Ob. Solo
tr
Vlns.
Vla.
Vc. Cb.

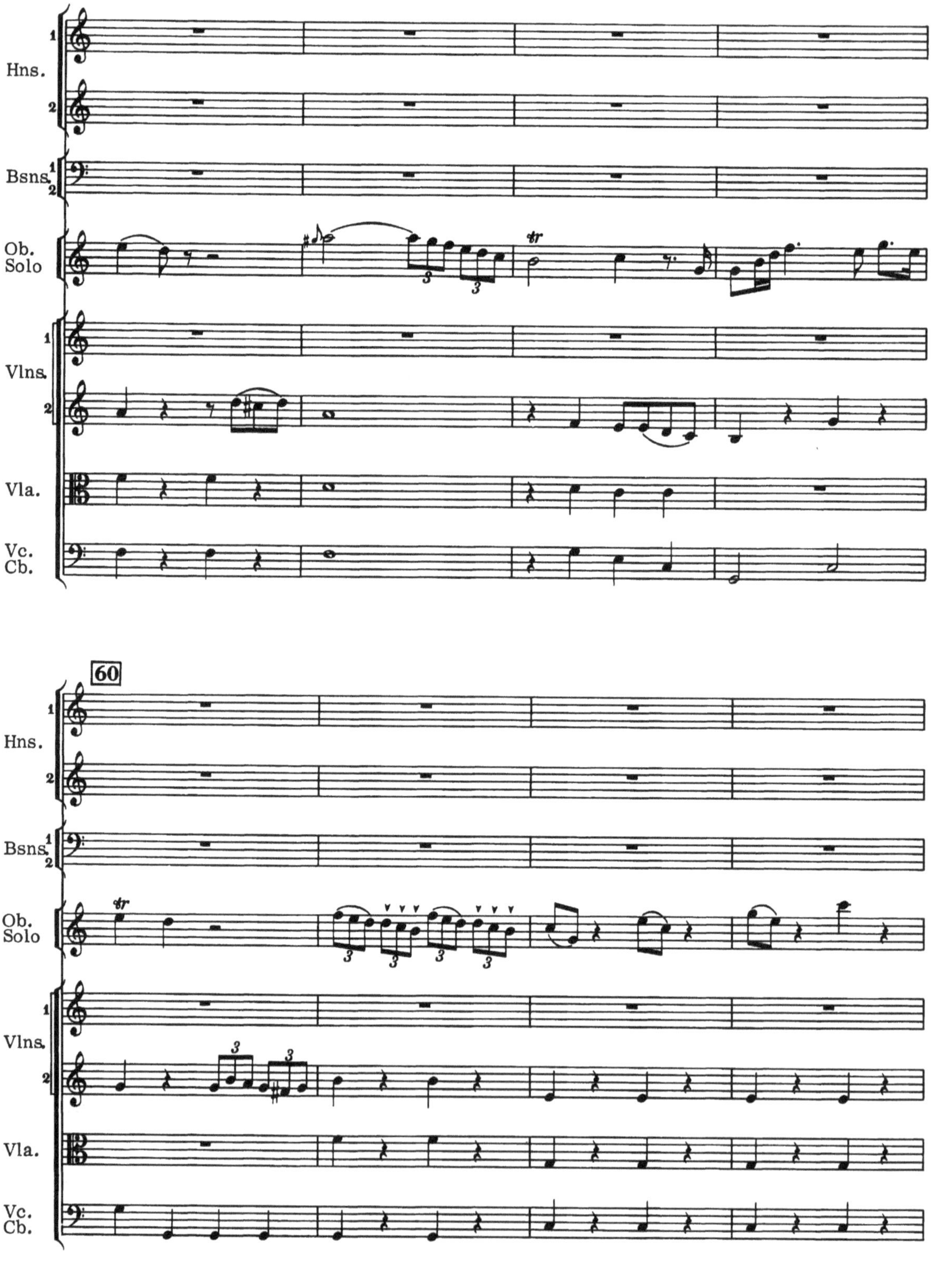
Hns.
Bsns.
Ob. Solo
Vlns.
Vla.
Vc. Cb.
60

65
Hns.
1
2
Bsns.
1
2
Ob. Solo
Vlns.
1
2
Vla.
Vc. Cb.
[fp]
fp
fp

70
Hns.
1
2
Bsns.
1
2
Ob. Solo
f
p
f
p
Vlns.
1
2
[f]
[p]
[f]
[p]
Vla.
f
p
f
p
Vc. Cb.
f
p
f
p

10

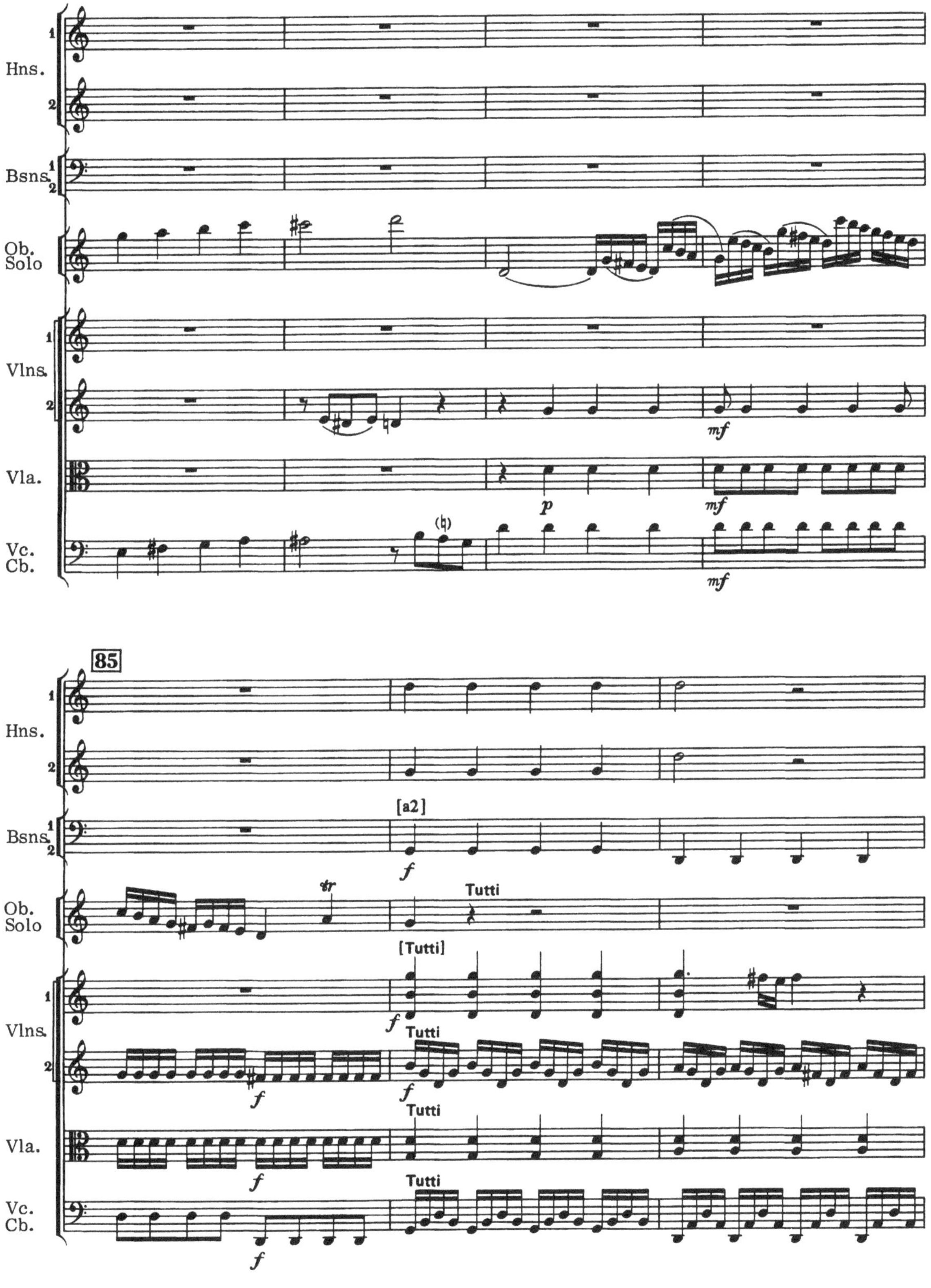

Hns.
1
2
Bsns.
Ob. Solo
Vlns.
Vla.
Vc. Cb.
mf
p
85
[a2]
f
tr
Tutti
[Tutti]

12

7. MS measure 89, Violin II part:    MS measure 89, Violin II obligato part:

8. MS shows E on third beat, with appogiatura on F above.

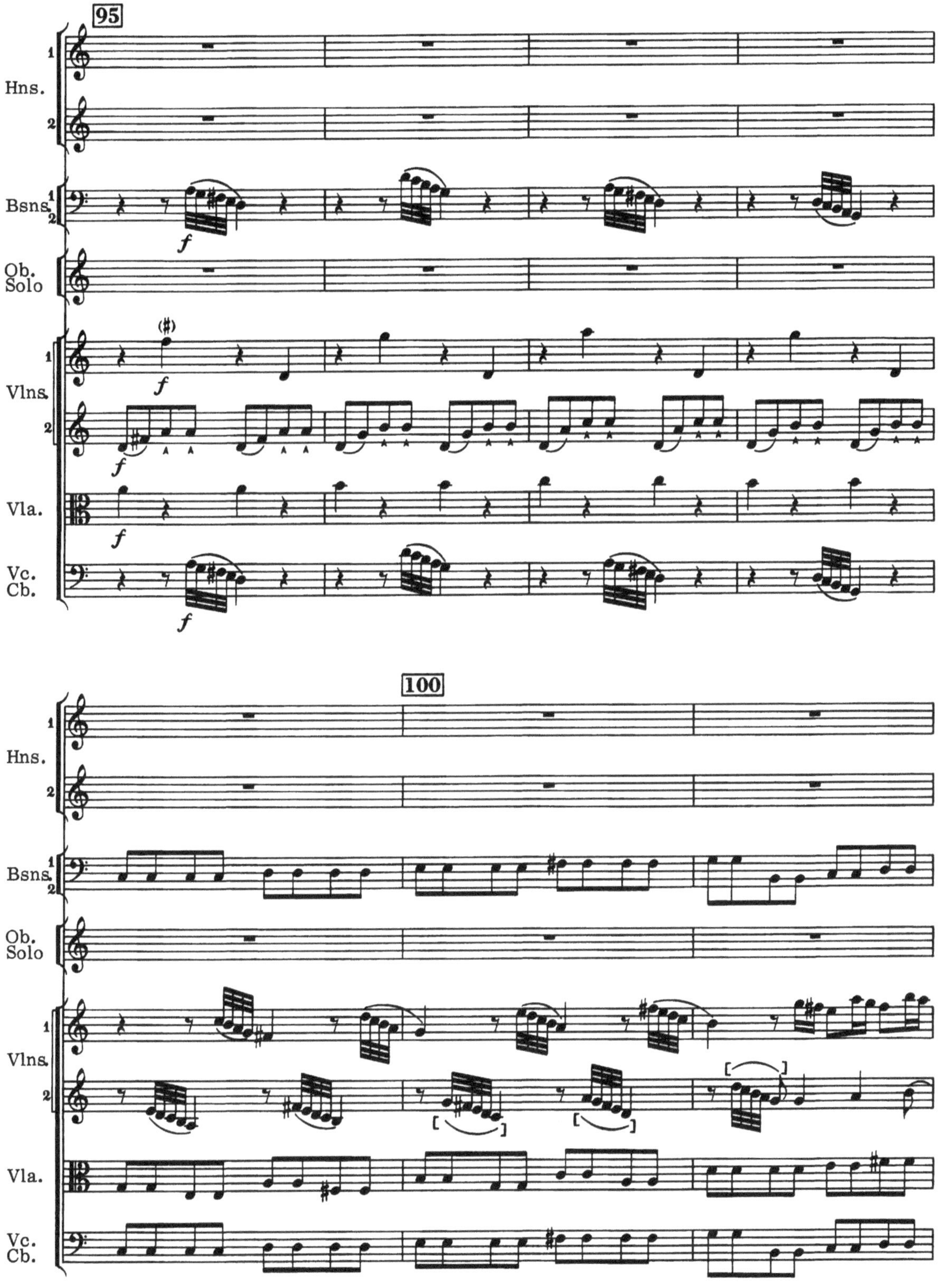
95
Hns. 1 2
Bsns. 1 2
Ob. Solo
Vlns. 1 2
Vla.
Vc. Cb.
f
100

**105**

9.

110
Hns.
Bsns.
Ob.
Solo
Vlns.
Vla.
Vc.
Cb.
f
Hns.
Bsns.
Ob.
Solo
Vlns.
Vla.
Vc.
Cb.
(♯)

10. MS Violin I, measure 116:

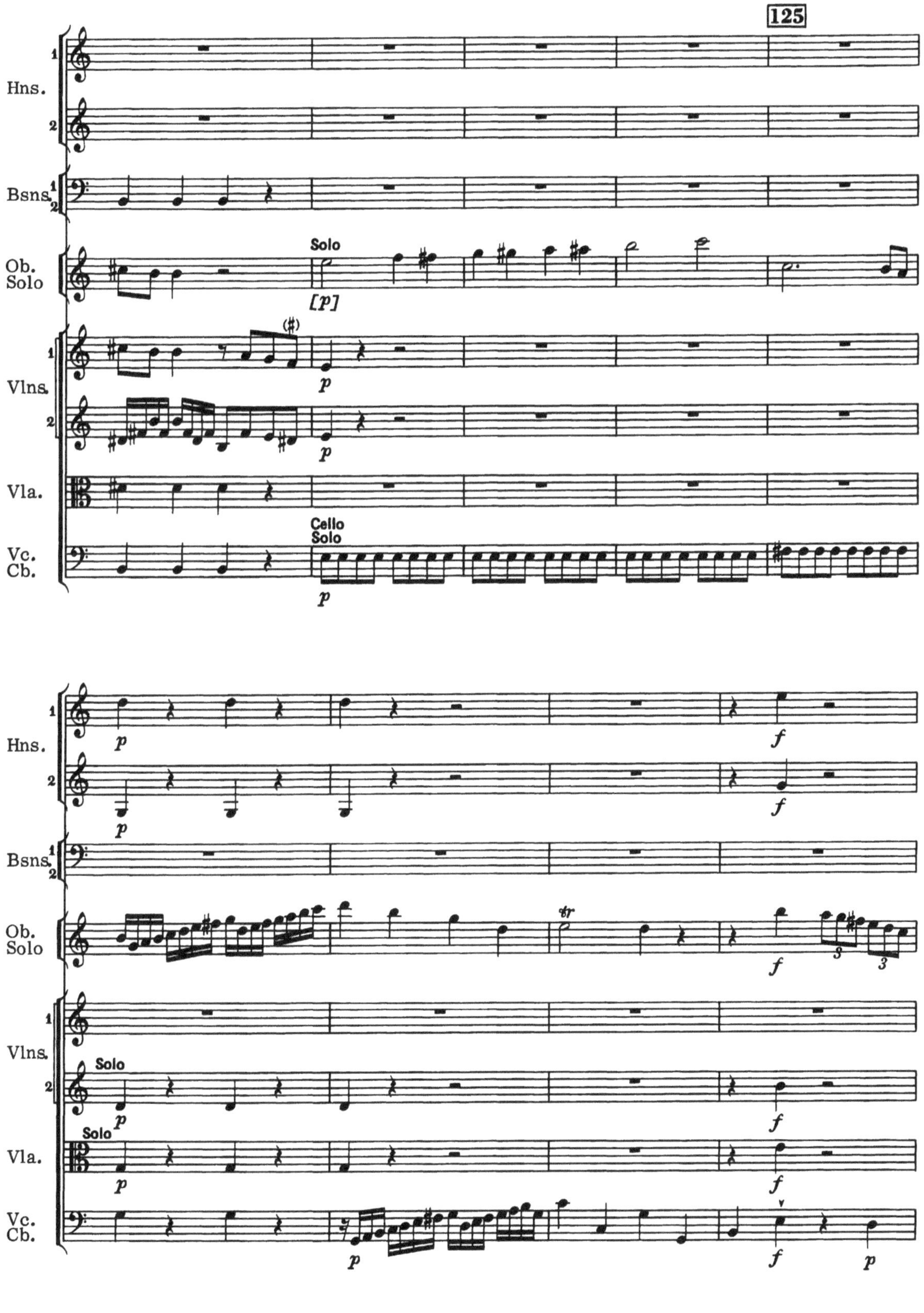
125
Hns.
Bsns.
Ob. Solo
Solo
[p]
Vlns.
Vla.
Cello Solo
Vc. Cb.
p
f
tr
3

18

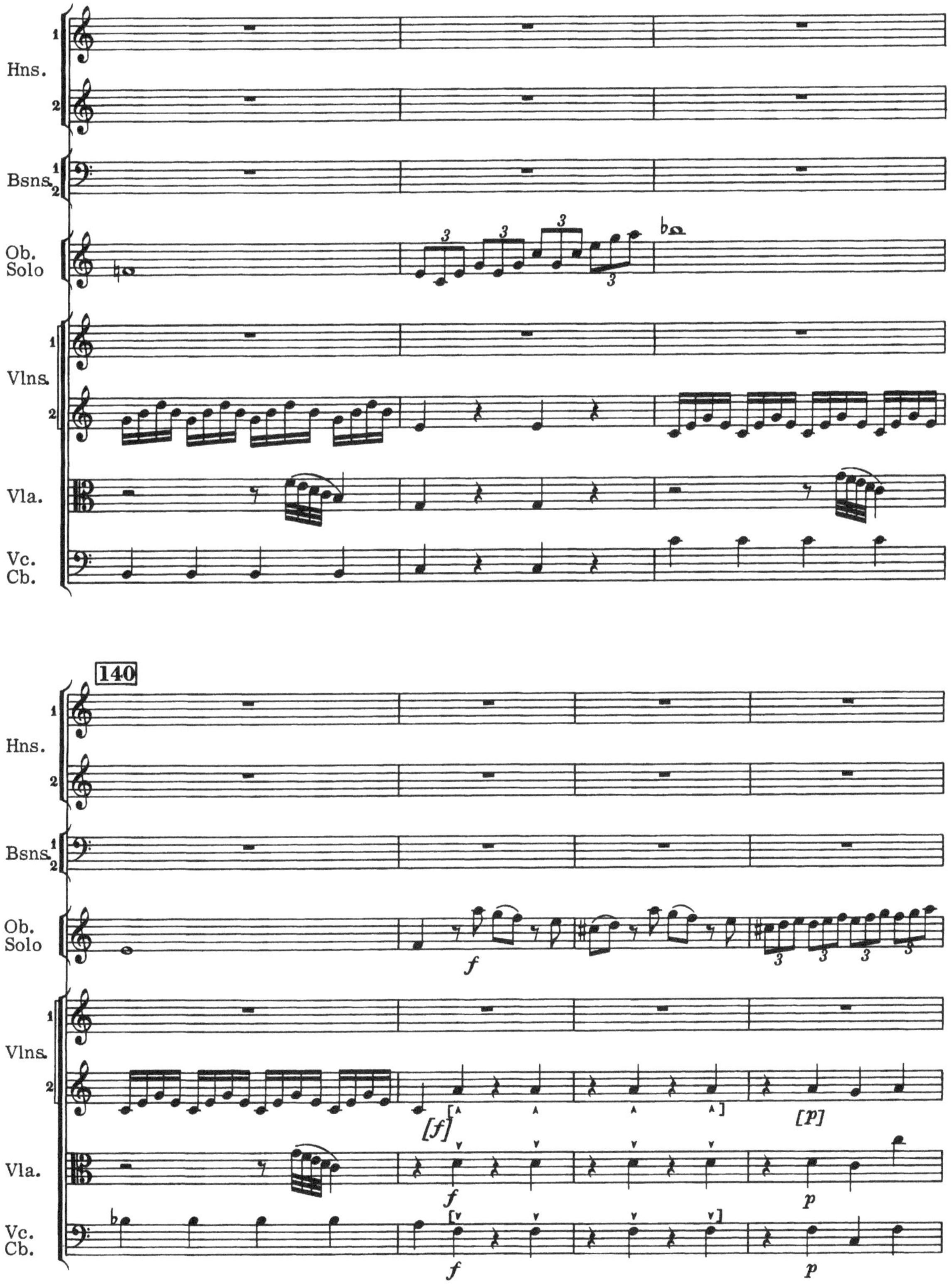
Hns.
Bsns.
Ob. Solo
Vlns.
Vla.
Vc. Cb.
140
f
[f]
[p]
p

145
Hns.
1
2
Bsns.
Ob.
Solo
tr
Tutti
f
Vlns.
[Tutti]
Vla.
[simile]
Vc.
Cb.
150
p

11. MS Violin I: "G" on ♪ of second beat.

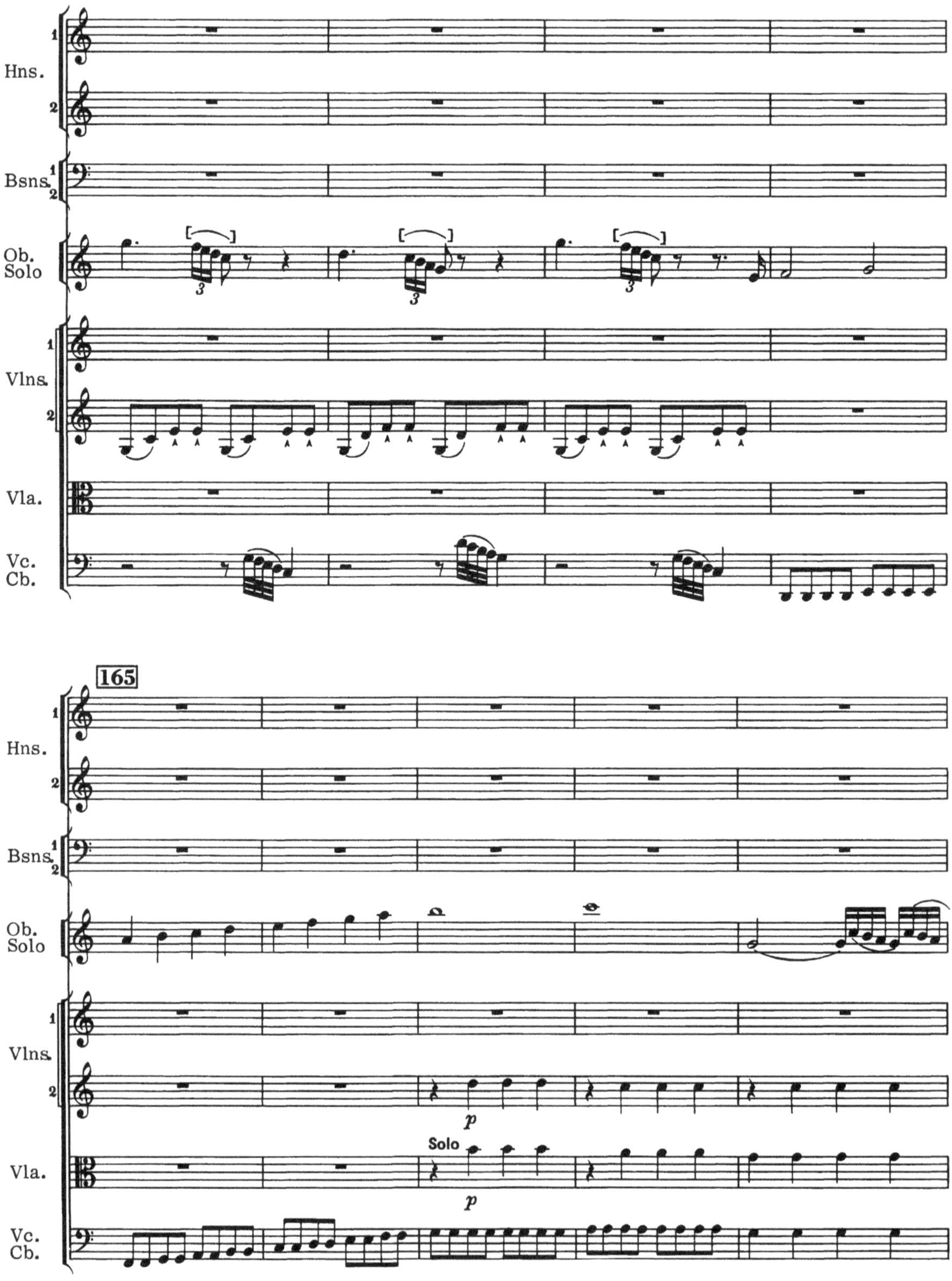
Hns.
Bsns.
Ob.
Solo
Vlns.
Vla.
Vc.
Cb.
165
Solo
p

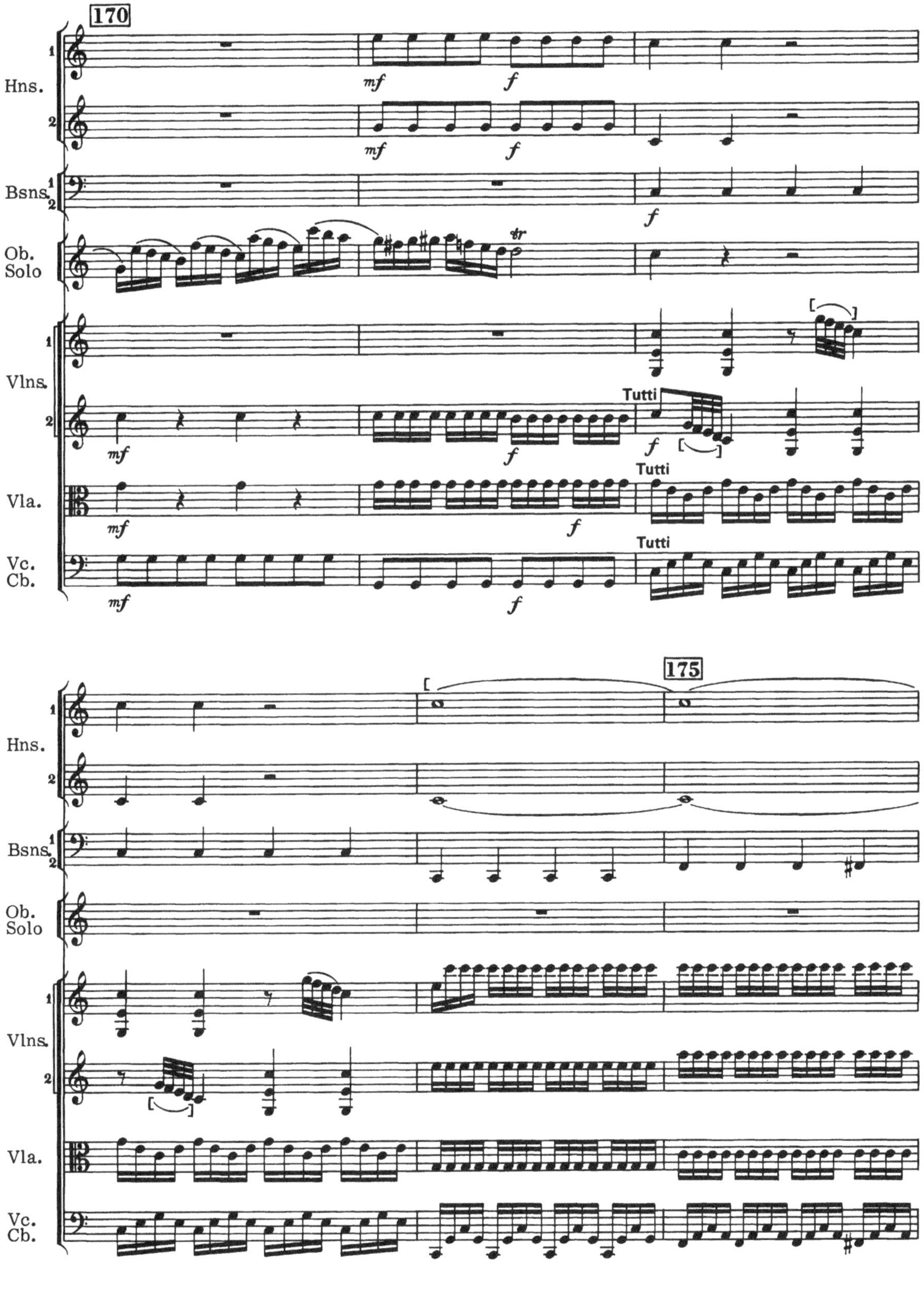
170
Hns.
1
2
Bsns.
Ob.
Solo
Vlns.
Vla.
Vc.
Cb.
mf
f
tr
Tutti
175

12. See explanation of these cadenzas in critical commentary.
13. This note is sustained softly by the Cellos.  MS shows a half-note rest for Basses.

14. MS Violin I, measures 181 and 182:

# II

15
Hns.
Bsns.
[a2]
f
Ob.
Solo
Vlns.
tr
3
Vlas.
Vc.
Cb.
20
[f]
Solo
[p]
p
Cello Solo

25
30
Hns.
Bsns.
Ob.
Solo
Vlns.
Vlas.
p
p
Vc.
Cb.
35
Hns.
Bsns.
Ob.
Solo
tr
Vlns.
Vlas.
[Tutti]
Vc.
Cb.

* MS has 𝆏 on 3rd beat.

*15.* Although not in the MS, an A-natural was probably played here.

30

## III

15
Hns.
[f]
[f]
Bsns.
Ob.
Solo
[f]
Vlns.
Vla.
Vc.
Cb.
20
Hns.
Bsns.
p
Ob.
Solo
Solo
[p]
Vlns.
Vla.
Cello
Solo
Vc.
Cb.
p

32

40
Hns.
1
2
[f]
[f]
Bsns.
1
2
[f]
Ob.
Solo
Tutti
sf
sf
sf
sf
Vlns.
1
2
f
Tutti
f
Vla.
f
Vc.
Cb.
f

45
Hns.
1
2
Bsns.
1
2
Ob.
Solo
Solo
[p]
tr
3
3
Vlns.
1
2
Solo
p
Vla.
Vc.
Cb.

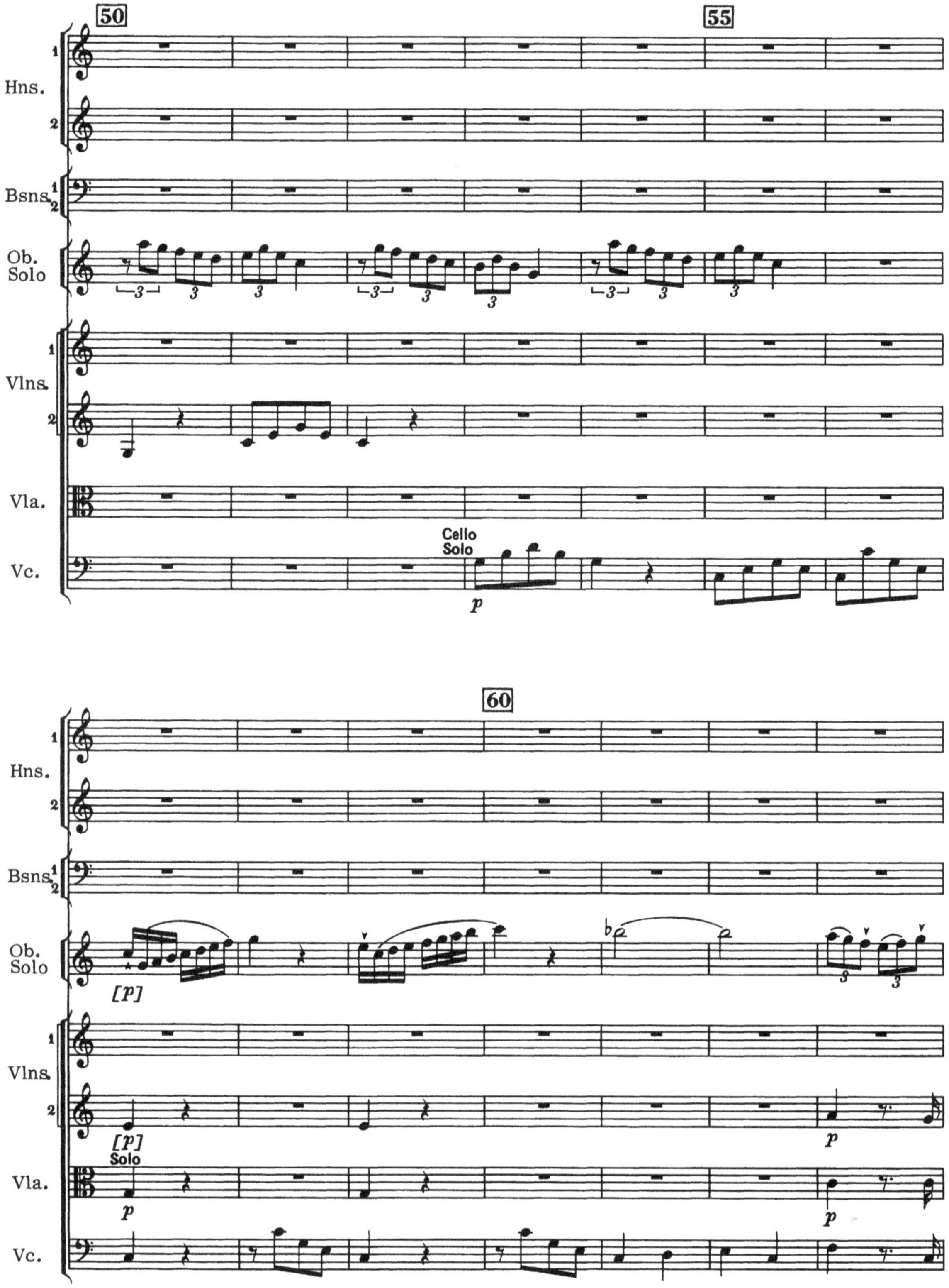
50
55
Hns.
Bsns.
Ob.
Solo
Vlns.
Vla.
Vc.
Cello
Solo
p
60
[p]
Solo

65
Hns.
1
2
Bsns.
1
2
[f]
Ob.
Solo
Tutti
[f]
Vlns.
1
[f]
2
Tutti
f
Vla.
Tutti
f
Vc.
Cb.
Tutti
f
70
75
[Solo]
[p]
Solo
p
Solo
p
Cello
Solo
p

80
Hns.
1
2
Bsns.
1
2
Ob.
Solo
Vlns.
1
2
Vla.
Vc.

85
Hns.
1
2
Bsns.
1
2
Ob.
Solo
Vlns.
1
2
Vla.
Vc.

16. A cadenza is not appropriate here.

38

17. MS Violin II obligato part, measure 108 and following:

115
Hns.
Bsns.
Ob. Solo
tr
Tutti
Vlns.
[f]
(♯)
[p]
[f]
f
Solo
Vla.
p
f
Vc.
f
120
125
Hns.
Bsns.
[f]
Ob. Solo
Vlns.
[f]
Tutti
f
Tutti
Vla.
f
Tutti
Vc. Cb.
f

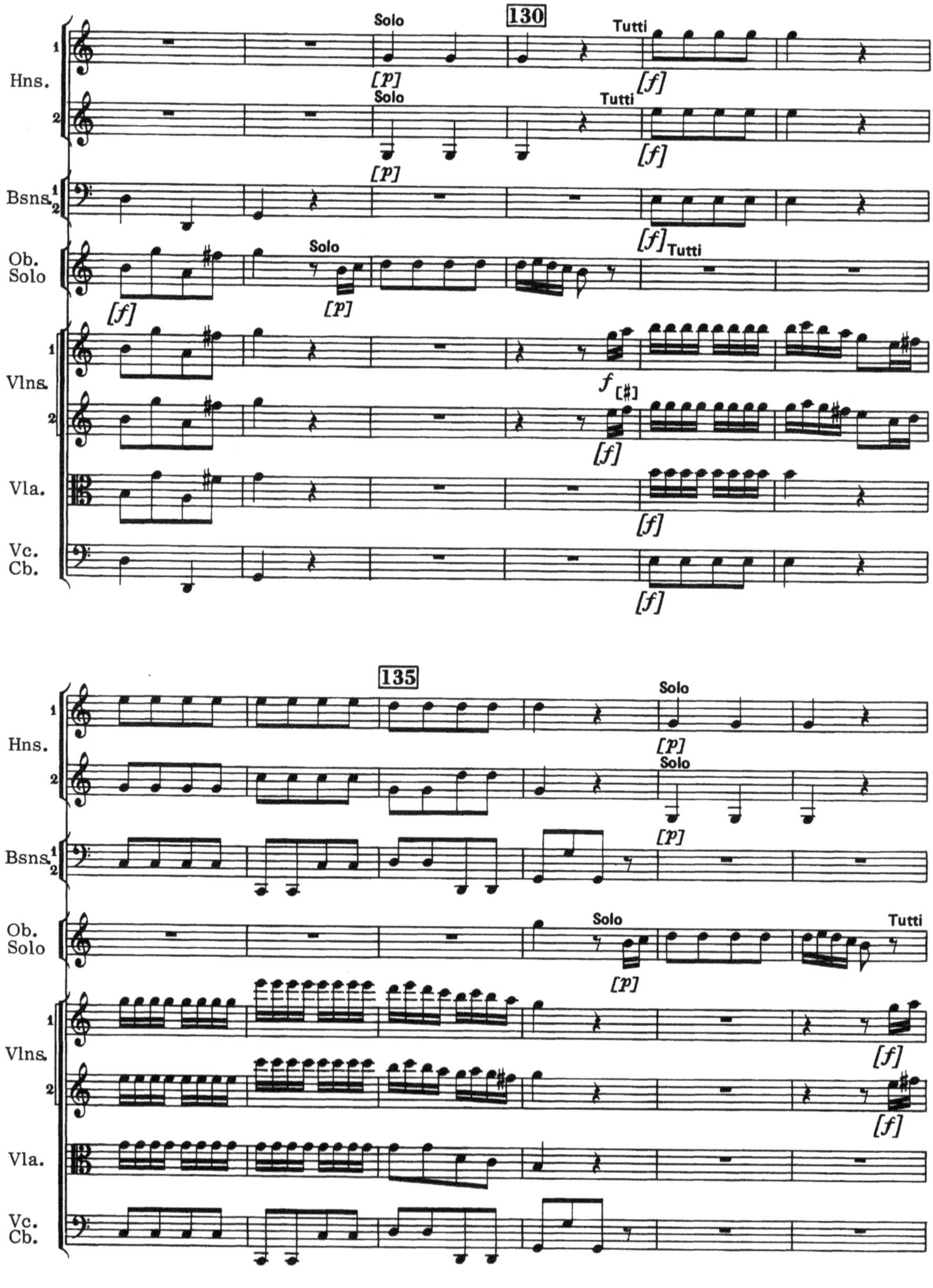
130
Hns.
Bsns.
Ob. Solo
Vlns.
Vla.
Vc. Cb.
Solo
Tutti
[p]
[f]
f
[♯]
135

18. MS measures 144-146, Violin II and obligato Violin II parts:

42

19. These six half-notes on E should probably be tied, in the same manner that
Herschel has tied the half-notes on G at measures 183-188.

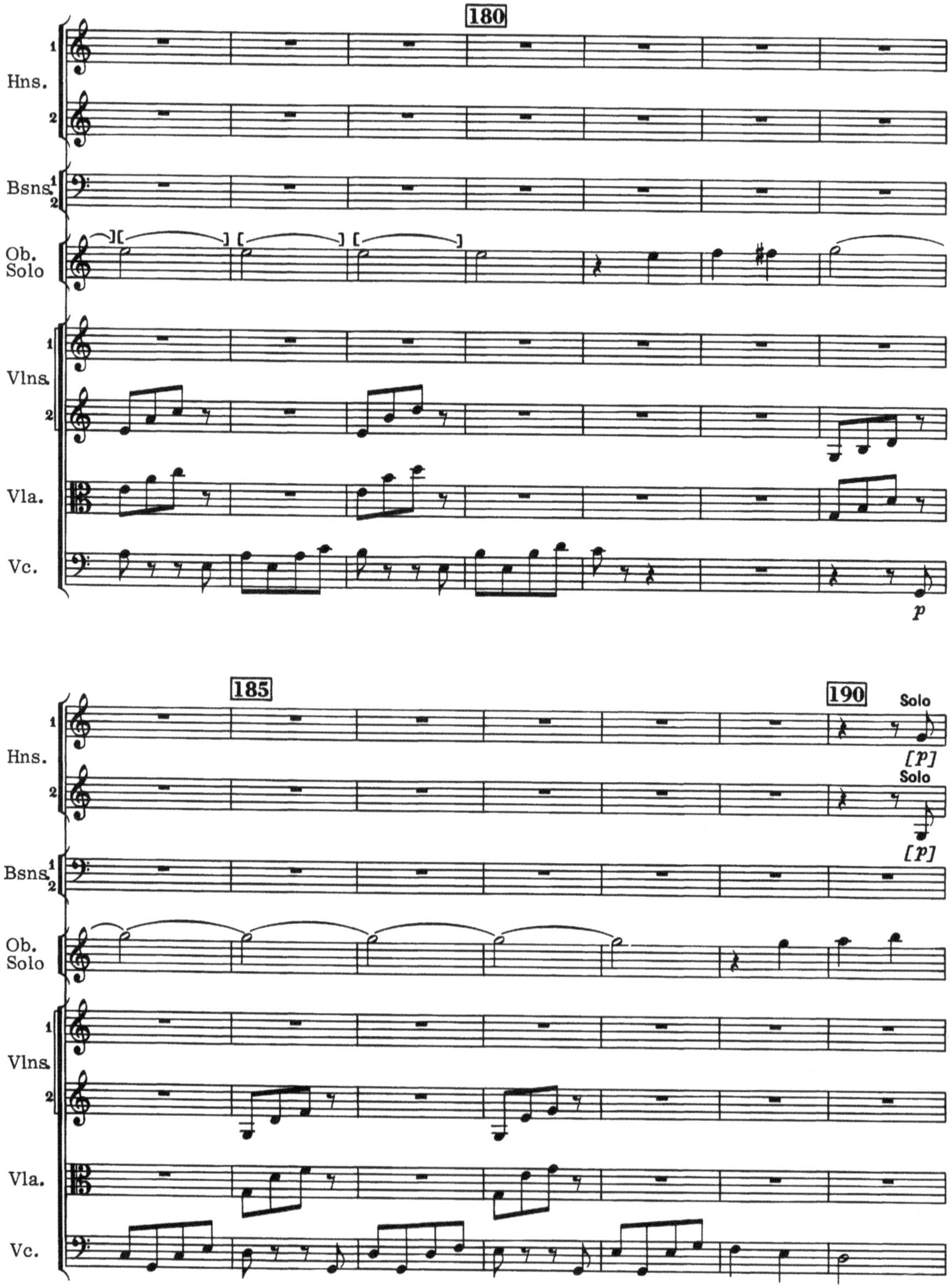

180
Hns.
Bsns.
Ob. Solo
Vlns.
Vla.
Vc.
p
185
190
Solo
[p]
Solo
[p]

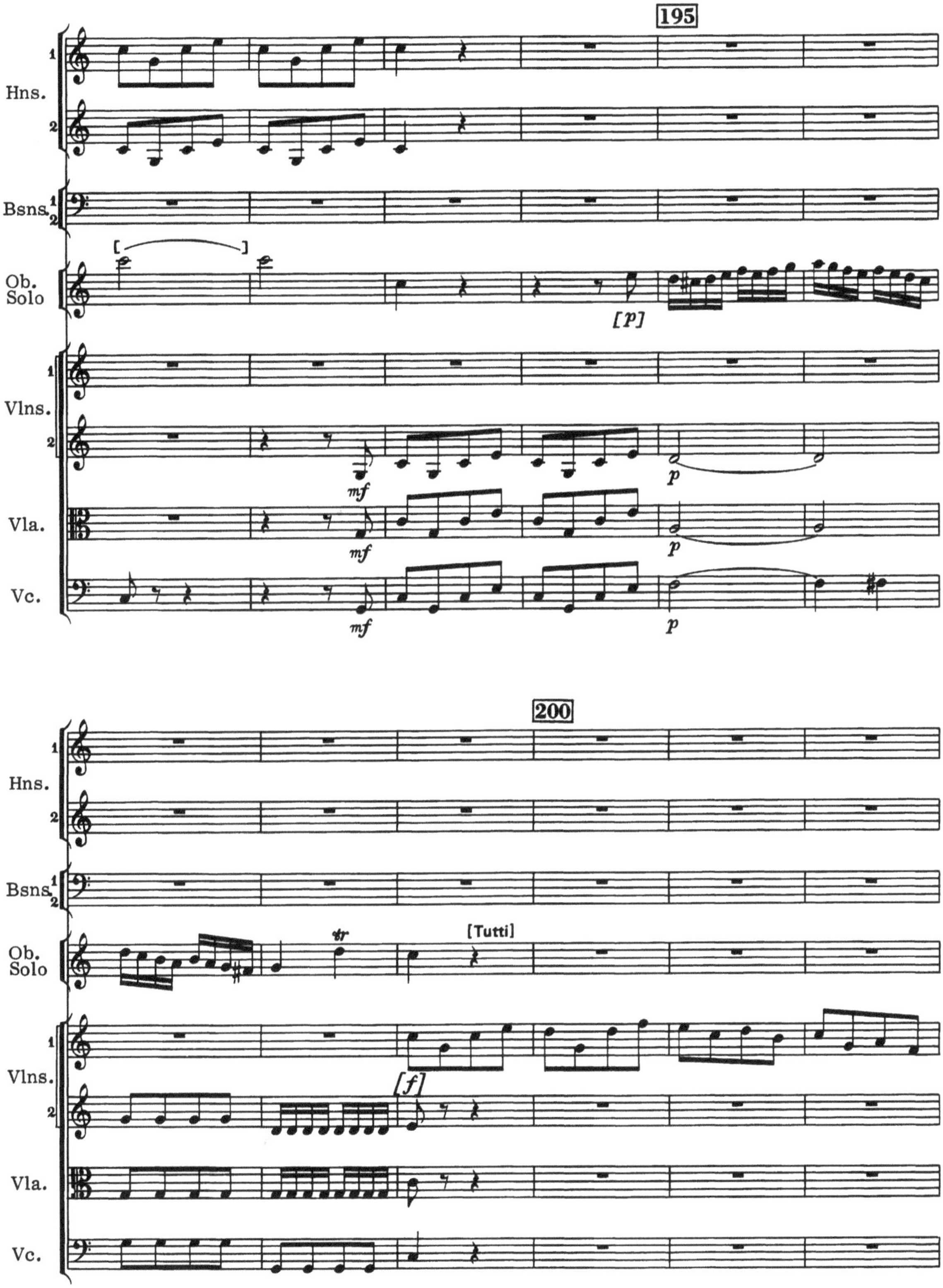
195
Hns.
Bsns.
Ob. Solo
[p]
Vlns.
mf
p
Vla.
Vc.
200
tr
[Tutti]
[f]

205
Hns.
Tutti
[Tutti]
[f]
f
Bsns.
Ob.
Solo
Vlns.
Vla.
Vc.
Cb.
210
215
Solo
[Solo]
[p]

220
Hns.
Bsns.
[f]
Ob.
Solo
[p]
Vlns.
f
Solo
[f]
p
Vla.
[f]
Vc.
Cb.
f
225
Hns.
Bsns.
Ob.
Solo
Vlns.
[mf]
[p]
Solo
Vla.
mf
p
Vc.
Cb.

48

49

20. MS measure 246: Solo Cello holds throughout cadenza until tutti (measure 247).

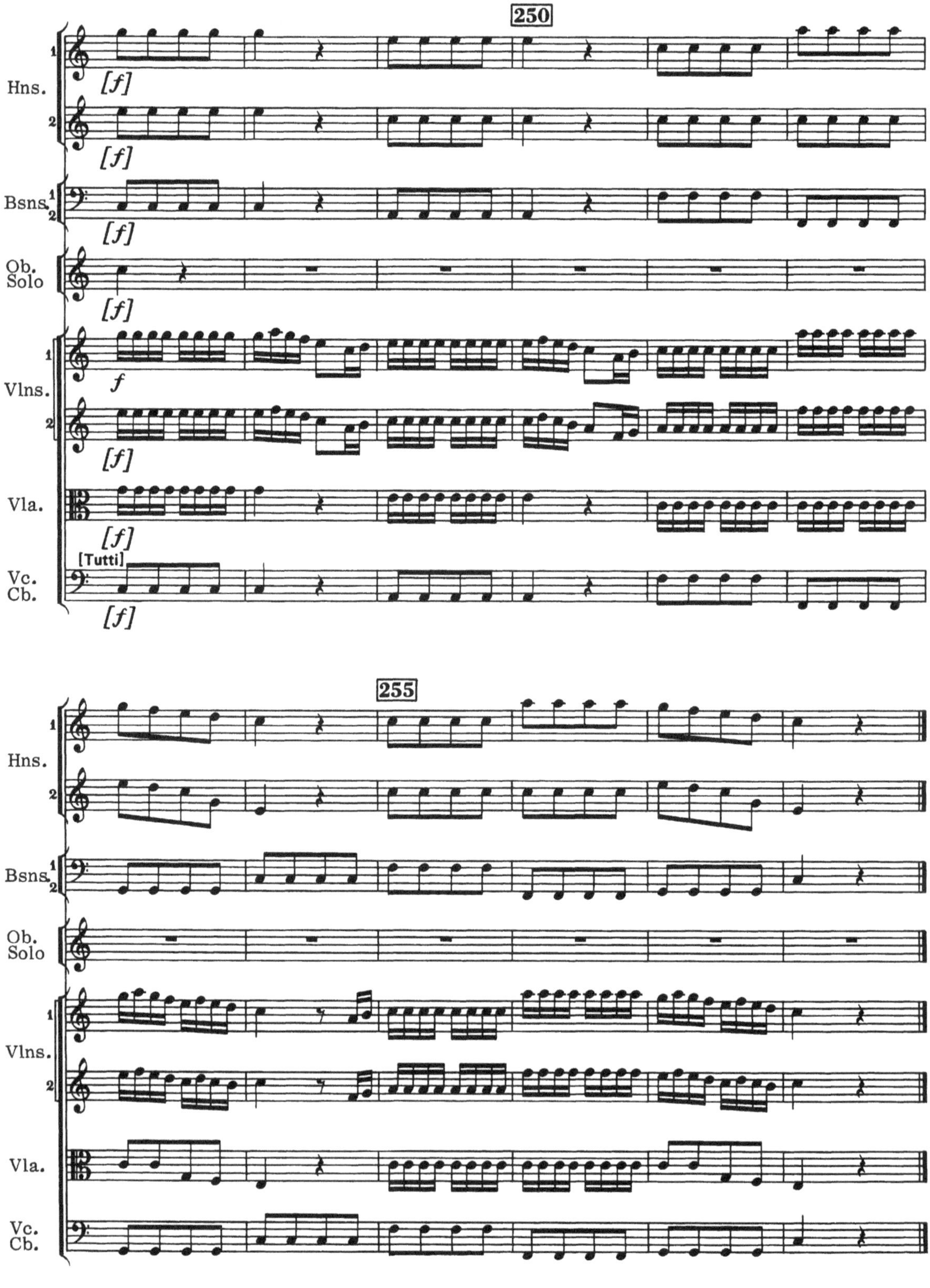
250
Hns. 1 2
[f]
Bsns. 1 2
Ob. Solo
Vlns. 1 2
f
Vla.
[Tutti]
Vc. Cb.
255

# MOVEMENT OF AN OBOE CONCERTO, IN C

William Herschel

*1.* Oboe may have played in unison with Violin I, measures 9-16.

15
Hns. 1 2
Ob. Solo
[Solo]
[mf]
Vlns. 1 2
Vla.
Vc. Cb.
[mf]
20
25
Hns. 1 2
[f]
Ob. Solo
tr
Vlns. 1 2
[f]
[f]
Vla.
[f]
Vc. Cb.
[f]

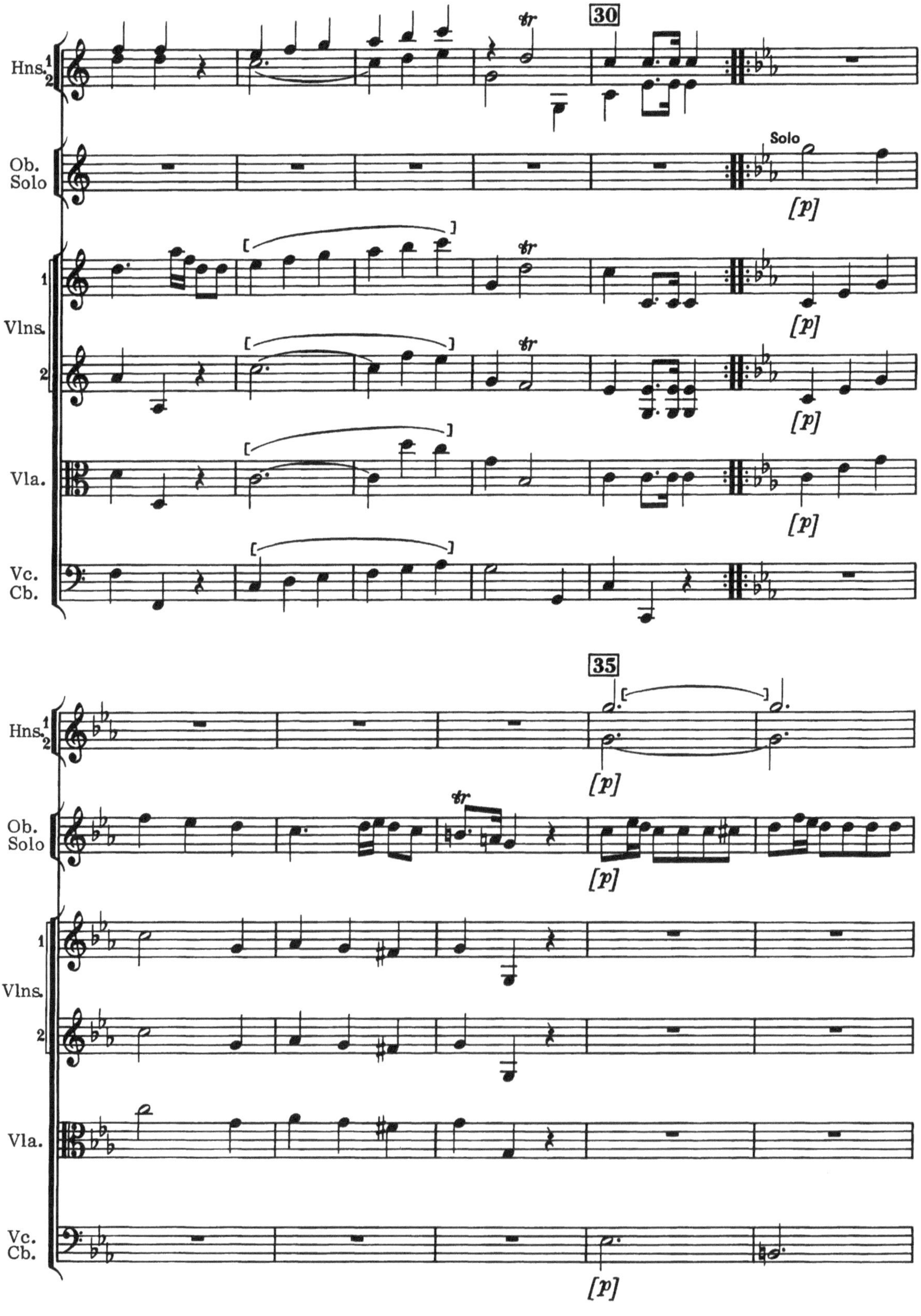
30
35
Hns. 1 2
Ob. Solo
Solo
Vlns. 1 2
Vla.
Vc. Cb.
tr
[p]

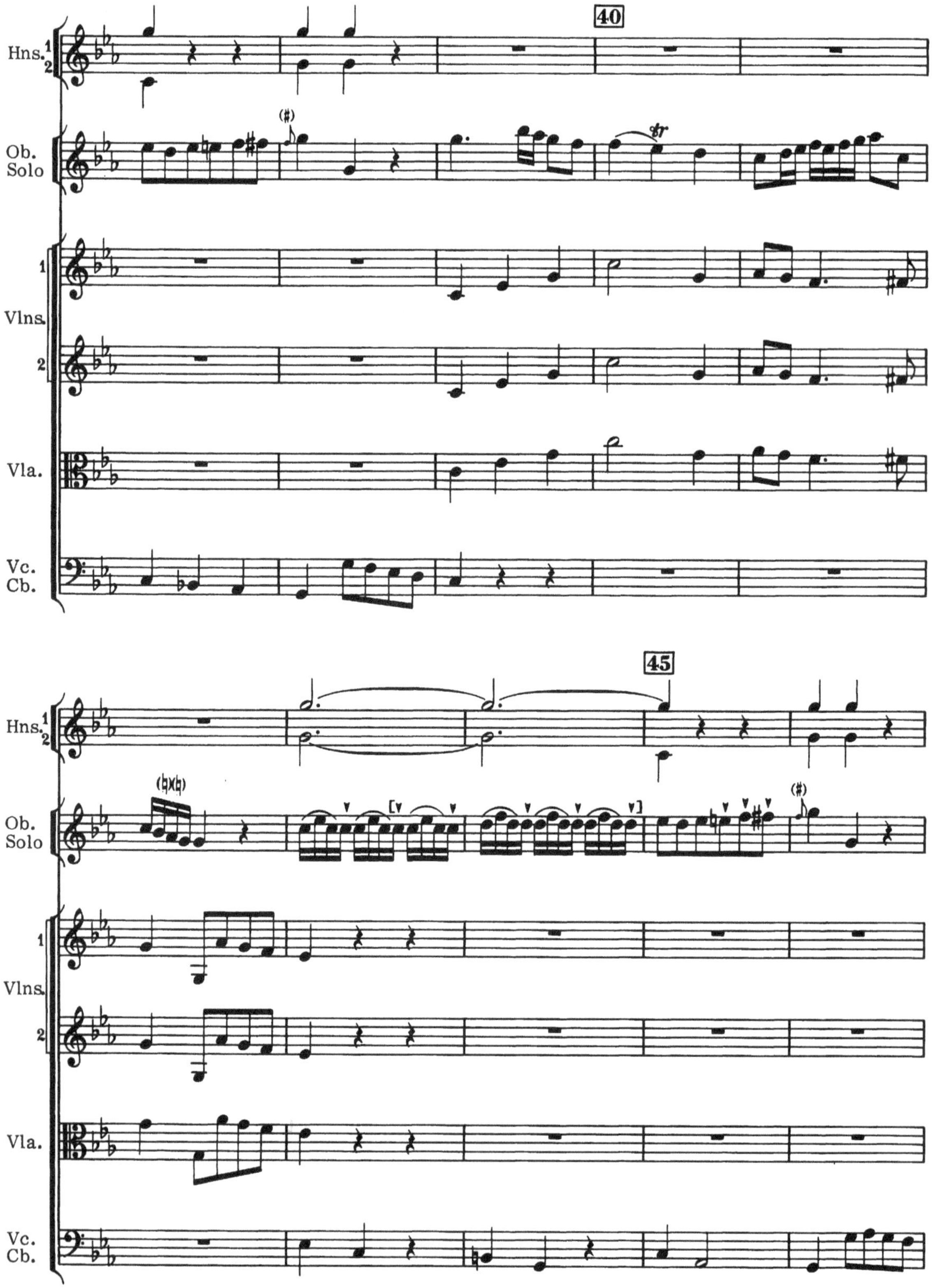
Hns. 1 2
Ob. Solo
Vlns. 1 2
Vla.
Vc. Cb.
40
tr
45

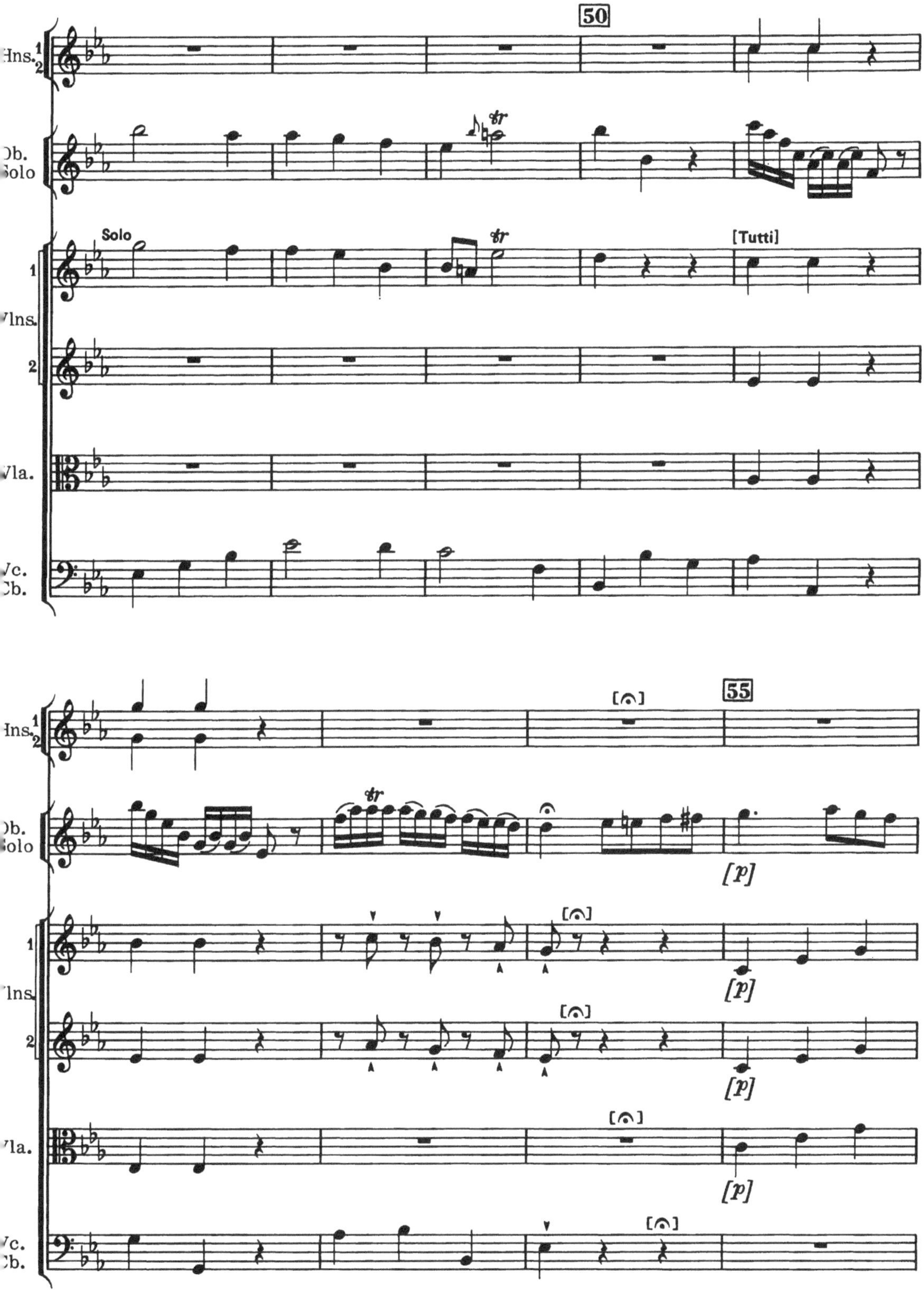
50
Solo
[Tutti]
tr
Vla.
55
[p]

60
Hns. 1 2
Ob. Solo
1
Vlns.
2
Vla.
Vc. Cb.
65
Hns. 1 2
Ob. Solo
(♮)
3
tr
[Solo]
[ 3 ]
tr
1
Vlns.
2
Vla.
Vc. Cb.

2. MS measure 73, Oboe:

8

3. Oboe may have played in unison with Violin I, measures 79-94.

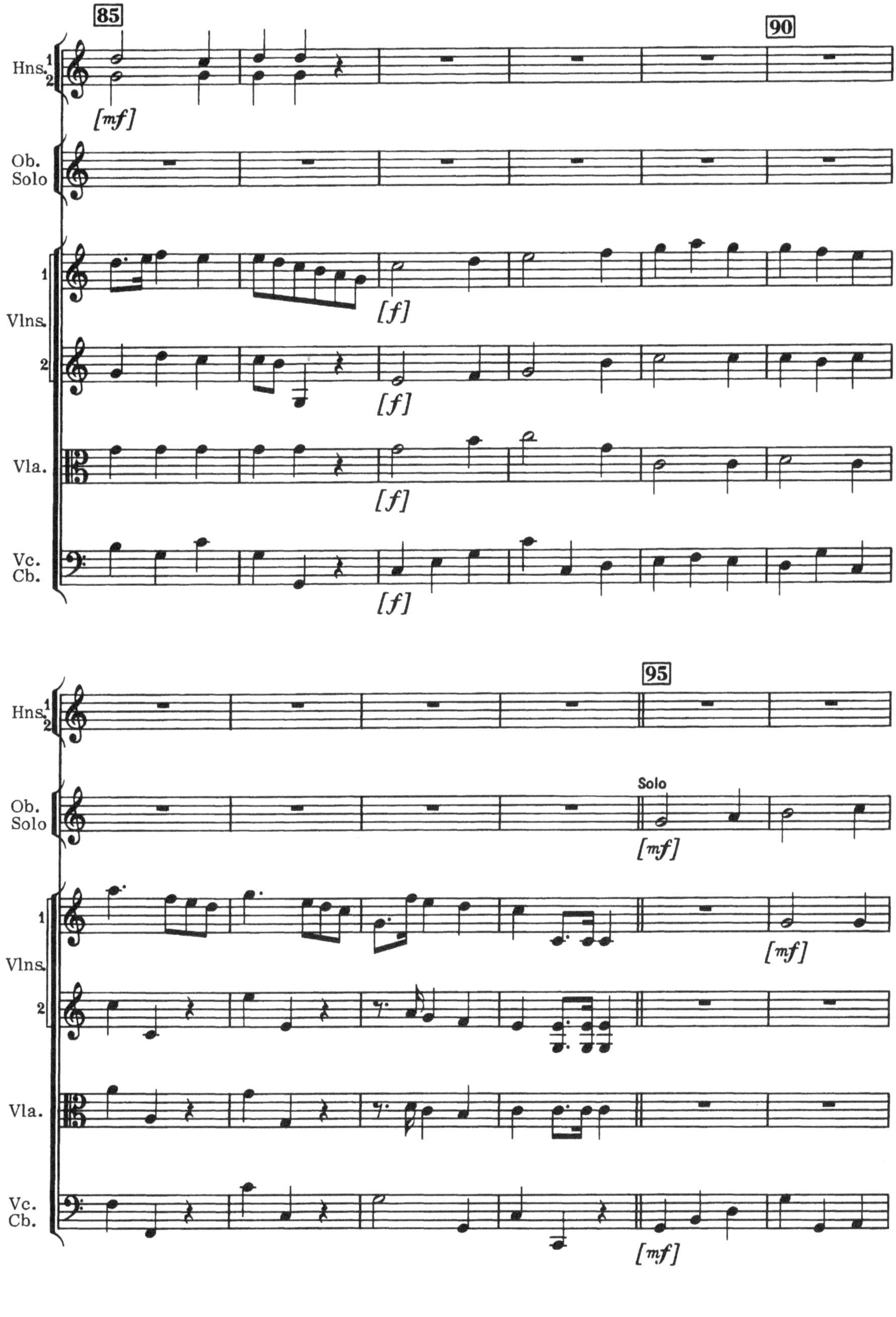
85
90
Hns. 1 2
[mf]
Ob. Solo
Vlns. 1 2
[f]
Vla.
Vc. Cb.
95
Solo
[mf]

4. Measure 107 is obliterated in Violin II and Viola parts; "primo" is written
here, probably referring to this pattern as first played at measure 29.

5. MS shows only first two beats in Horn parts at measure 115; editor has added the remaining
notes to coincide with the same Horn pattern at measures 131-132, 143-144, 157-158 and 161-162.

6. MS measures 117-124 shows only Violin I, with notation "Come Primo".
Editor used measures 87-94, though measures 9-16 could also be considered "Come Primo".

12

7. MS: "Come Primo", with measures 133-140 containing only Violin I part.
Editor chose to repeat measures 9-16 here; measures 87-94 could also have been used.

8. MS: "Come Primo", with measures 149-154 containing only Violin I part.
Editor chose to repeat measures 25-30 here.

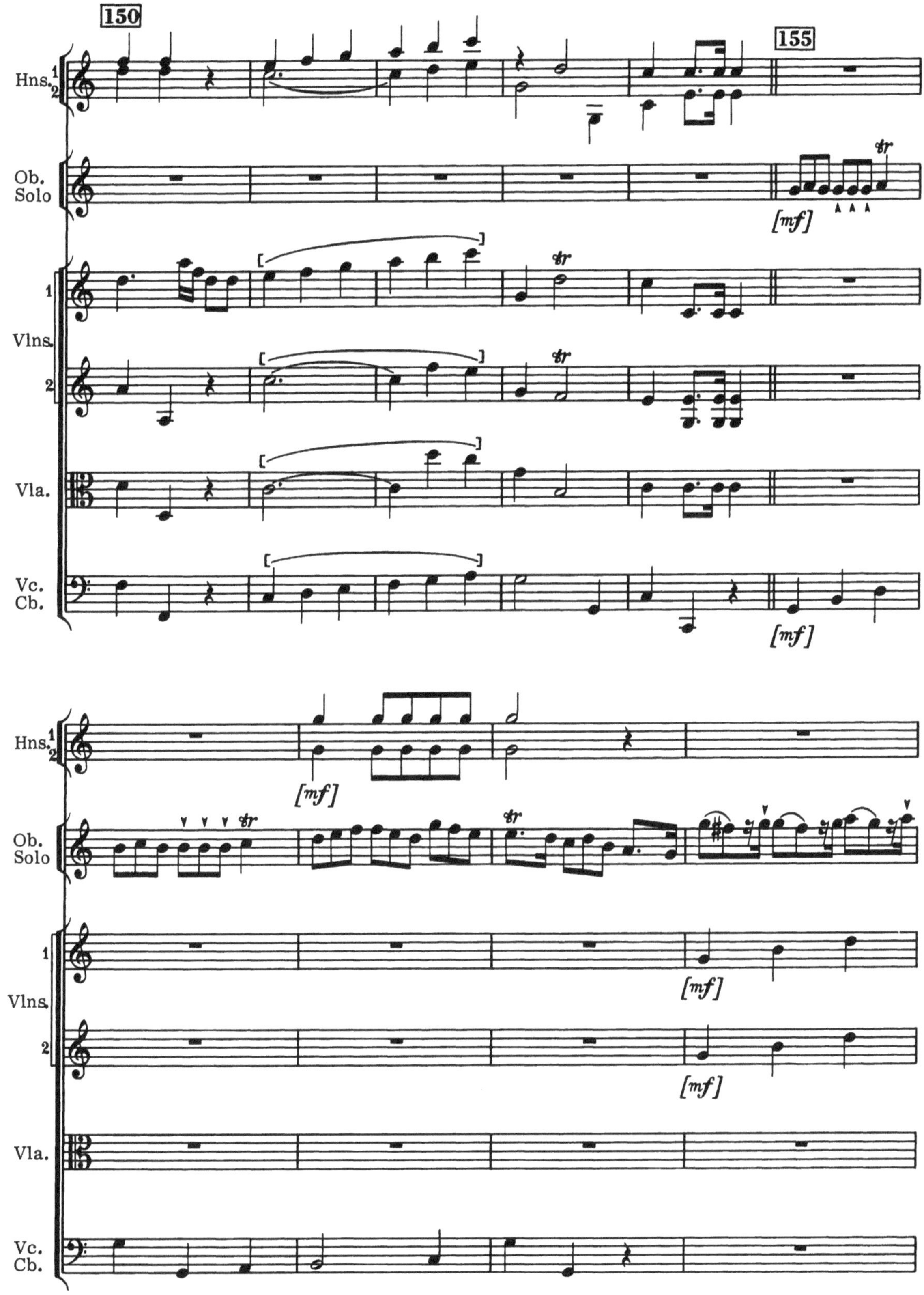
150
155
Hns. 1 2
Ob. Solo
Vlns. 1 2
Vla.
Vc. Cb.
[mf]
tr

9. MS measure 166, Violin I, first beat: "G".

www.ingramcontent.com/pod-product-compliance
Lightning Source LLC
Chambersburg PA
CBHW080927100426
42812CB00007B/2397

* 9 7 8 0 8 7 1 6 9 2 2 5 2 *